How
Big
Is
God?

HIGHTOWER BOOKS

By Charlotte Huskey

authorHOUSE®

AuthorHouse™
1663 Liberty Drive
Bloomington, IN 47403
www.authorhouse.com
Phone: 1 (800) 839-8640

Published by AuthorHouse 06/30/2016

ISBN: 978-1-5246-1430-0 (sc)
ISBN: 978-1-5246-1429-4 (e)

Print information available on the last page.

Scripture quotations marked KJV are from the Holy Bible, King James Version
(Authorized Version). First published in 1611. Quoted from the KJV Classic
Reference Bible, Copyright © 1983 by The Zondervan Corporation.

Scripture quotations marked NKJV are taken from the New King James Version.
Copyright © 1982 by Thomas Nelson, Inc. Used by permission. All rights reserved.

This book is printed on acid-free paper.

The purpose of this book is "That the generation to come might know [God's laws and works], even the
children which should be born; who should arise and declare them to their children: That they may
set their hope in God, and not forget the works of God, but keep his commandments." Psalms 78:6, 7

This book is available on Amazon and in Christian book distributors worldwide.
Contact information:
Charlotte Huskey
811 Foster Road
Guthrie, OK 73044
email: charlottenellhuskey@gmail.com
Facebook Charlotte Huskey
www.wiseeyes.net

This book is dedicated to Harland Smith and to all parents who desire to build their children's faith in God.

At the age of 23, lying in his Navy bunk bed one night during World War II, my father, Harland Smith, responded to the loving conviction of the Holy Spirit and gave his life to the Lord. From that point on he was a missionary at heart and spent his life spreading and sharing the Gospel story. I remember as a small boy, he would stop the car and ask young boys playing alongside the road if they went to Sunday school. On Sunday mornings we would make several stops, picking up boys to attend his Sunday school class. Dad would never miss an opportunity to witness to outright strangers. His zeal was born of a burning love for the salvation of souls.

He was a humble man who was not self-focused and who did not have an exaggerated opinion of himself. That was always apparent. He taught me that we should not put ourselves on display in any way but to stay hidden behind the cross of Christ, that He was the center and focus of all we do. That was Dad. That was a constant theme in his life.

His last years were devoted to spreading the gospel in Baja California, Mexico. There were many, many memories and experiences of those years. One that stood out to me was when he told about preparing for morning service out behind a rock amongst the desert landscape, praying for God's blessing and anointing. He prayed, "God, I want the very best from you this morning!" He said, God spoke right back and said, "And I want the very best from you!"

That is what Dad would say to all of us today. Give your very best to God!

Clifford Smith

Harland Smith

CONTENTS

GOD'S WAY IS BEST

"God's way is best; if human wisdom
A fairer way may seem to show,
Tis' only that our earth-dimmed vision
The truth can never clearly know.

"Had I the choosing of my pathway,
In blindness I would go astray,
And wander far away in darkness
Nor reach that land of endless day

"He leadeth true; I will not question,
Tho' through the valley I shall go,
Tho' I should pass through clouds of trial,
And drink the cup of human woe.

"God's way is best; heart, cease thy struggling
To see and know and understand;
Forsake thy fears and doubts, but trusting,
Submit thyself into His hand.

"Thy way is best, so lead me onward,
My all I give to Thy control;
Thy loving hand will truly guide me,
And safe to glory bring my soul.

"God's way is best, I will not murmur,
Although the end I may not see;
Where'er He leads I'll meekly follow–
God's way is best, is best for me."

C. W. Naylor

Sometimes we are annoyed about situations that arise; however, later we realize these circumstances helped us learn and grow into better people. Our family would not have chosen to experience the unbelievable, but true, incidents in this book; although, these circumstances strengthened our faith and taught us that God's way is always best.

INTRODUCTION

This book is a compilation of true life events experienced by a young couple who dared to follow God's leading. James and Charlotte Huskey's faith and confidence in God was deep. They did not hesitate to obey God's call to the mission field. This decision led them through many dangerous, yet exciting adventures.

Charlotte gives a first-hand account of how God supplied needs when it seemed impossible. She tells about James' arrest, of emergencies with no way to send for help and how they were stranded in a burning desert. She relates how God miraculously healed their bodies, sent them help and provisions just in time, and directed their lives.

This book is an excellent resource for parents who desire to build their children's faith. At the end of each episode there are questions for discussion. Children will look forward to family worship time. It will provide an excellent opportunity to help them see that God's way is truly best for their lives also.

Nelda Sorrell

These are the four main characters in this book along with their father James Albert Huskey, Harland Smith, and their mother, Charlotte, who wrote the stories. From left to right: James Robert (Bobby), Timothy Leon (Tim), Patricia Coleen (Tricia), and Rosa Maria (Rosi). This picture was taken in March 1961. The shirt Bobby has on was one of his surprise birthday gifts.

One Saturday morning after Brother and Sister Hite and Brother Smith had left to go to Mexico for the weekend, we felt it was time to act. We put gas into both our 1950 Chevy station wagon and this 1952 Chevy panel truck, where our belongings had been stored for three months, and we started off to Mexico.

Contact these children on Facebook and learn what they are doing today.

Moving to Baja

I am with you alway, even unto the end of the world.
Matthew 28:20b

I slammed on the brakes and bit my lip to suppress a scream, as a black station wagon swept in front of me, slowed almost to a stop, and made a left turn. Momentarily, I lost sight of the brown Chevy panel truck that my husband, James, was driving ahead of me. He was guiding me through the maze of narrow, pothole-filled streets of Tijuana. I had heard people joke about Tijuana drivers, but I never dreamed it would be this scary.

It was my first time driving in this Mexican City, just south of San Diego, California. Besides that, I was maneuvering through rush hour traffic with only one free hand. I was holding our ten-month-old daughter, Rosi, on my left shoulder. She had just cried herself to sleep. If I stopped to lay her down, I'd lose my guide and be stranded.

It was nearly six o'clock Friday evening, February 23, 1962. Heavy, dark rain clouds were causing darkness to set in early as I continued dodging potholes and wild drivers for another hour. Now that the lights of the city were behind us, all I could see were my guide's tail-lights. Often they disappeared around hairpin curves or dipped into dry creek beds. Nevertheless, the darkness was a blessing in disguise.

We were not just going on a mission trip with hopes of being back home soon to our usual life. We were leaving behind our families, friends, and all the comforts of the United States of America, and we were planning to live in Mexico for years to come. To make matters worse, we had only $10.00 and not a promise of another penny. Perhaps Baby Rosi's crying was because she had sensed how tense and emotional I was as we were passing through all the check points while crossing the international border.

An hour later, at about 8:00 p.m., James pulled off the highway beside a tiny, deserted looking house that was surrounded by knee-high grass and weeds. He came back to my car and said, "Well, this is the place. Let's just sleep in the cars till morning."

"Okay. Just tell me, where is the bathroom? We need to go."

"Well, well—it's right there, that little shanty. Here's the flash light."

I shivered, partly from the cold, and partly from what I might find in that creaky outhouse. I thought we had come to the end of the earth. There was not a light anywhere. Surely if there were houses around, we could at least see a candlelight. There was only darkness. I put Rosi in the back seat beside her brother, Tim, who had turned two just one week before. They snuggled together. While she was sleeping, Tricia, my four year old, and I went to the outhouse, and with my flashlight I surveyed its interior. There were spider webs in

2

the corners which were full of dead flies, so I knew fat spiders were lurking somewhere in the darkness. But the spiders were not as bad as the stench. Tricia, our little princess, covered her nose and cried. I hugged her while my tears were dropping on her blond hair. Back in the car, I held her tight until she fell asleep. Then, as I listened to the rain beating on the metal roof of our 1950 Chevy station wagon, a thousand thoughts were racing through my mind.

What had we gotten ourselves into? Were we completely crazy? I had promised James I'd be a missionary with him. How could I go back on my promise? The evening he proposed to me, we were standing on a pier at Redondo Beach, California, looking out over the Pacific Ocean, when he asked, "Will you marry me and go with me across the ocean?" The evening was so romantic as we listened to the hum of the waves on the rocks and watched the moon reflecting on the water. It sounded so exciting. "Yes," I had answered.

I envisioned the two of us boarding a ship while our family and near friends were standing on the dock giving us a big send-off. People in the church would be behind us with their blessings and financial support. We would have money for travel expenses and other basic needs. We married a year later on December 26, 1954, at my home church in Jefferson, Oregon. Now, eight years later, we were going to the mission field together with our four children.

James was parts manager at Lambert's Chevrolet for several years and was earning a good salary. The year before we moved, he had received honors from General Motors for increasing the volume of sales in Lambert's dealership more than any other dealership in that area of Northern California. It was very hard for James to leave this job and the security it afforded his family.

I fought many spiritual battles. I walked the floor trying to die to my dreams; the future of my children (their education, etc.), a comfortable home, orchard, and vegetable gardens. To leave this home seemed as bad as having my teeth pulled. By God's grace I was able to consecrate everything to God. We rented our nice new home for the amount of the mortgage payment, sold everything we didn't need, and quietly started for Mexico.

Where was the send-off I had imagined? Where was the mission station to which we should go if we needed help? We had already promised our only money ($10.00) to the owner as rent for the tiny house we were now parked behind.

We had been confused about where to go. Some church mission leaders advised going to El Alamo while others thought we should move to Santa Catarina. Both of these stations had a small mission house. We became desperate after two months of waiting on God to direct us while we were staying in a cabin at the Church of God Campground in Pacoima and in the homes of friends. James began fasting and praying. He went up to the mountain to hear from God. Three days later he came back and said, "God wants us in Rosarito."

"Where?" I asked.

"Rosarito," he answered.

Geneva Hite, the friend in whose home we were staying, spoke up. "We have been praying that God would send someone there. The Esquier family has just moved there and they need someone to disciple them. Here, I'll show you where it is." She got her Mexico map and spread it on the table. "There it is," she said, "right on the ocean. The government has just built a hydro-electric plant out at the edge of town. Many people from Southern Mexico are moving to Rosarito. It will be the perfect place to spread the gospel." She was so excited; I had to believe that God had really spoken. However, this night of our arrival, I was again wondering.

Brother Bill and Sister Geneva Hite made regular weekend mission trips from Pomona, California, down into the desert of Baja California with Brother Harland Smith. James had gone with them a couple of times and stayed in Rosarito so he could

4

find a house for us. Nothing had turned up except the possibility of this little shanty for $10.00 a month. It was located three miles north of downtown Rosarito Beach, Baja California. During this time, we were also hoping that some offerings would come in for our move to the mission field but no offerings came.

We were restless by now. Living with four children whose ages were five and under isn't exactly a piece of cake, especially when living in another person's home. Children are naturally prone to accidents, and they are curious. I was busy from morning until night keeping them out of things or cleaning up after them. We knew where to go, but we didn't know how to get there without money.

One Saturday morning after Brother and Sister Hite and Brother Smith had left for the weekend, we felt it was time to act. As we were wondering what we should do, the children found money while playing on a discarded sofa in the Hite's back yard. We took that as a sign that God would supply our needs. With this money, we put gas into our station wagon and into the mission's panel truck (where our belongings were stored) and started out. How different all this was from what I had envisioned that night on the pier when I had promised James that I would be a missionary with him.

Instead of floating on an ocean liner, I was cramped up in a car trying to sleep to the tune of rain dropping on the metal car roof. Sometime in the wee hours of the morning, I dozed off.

Questions for Discussion:
1. To where was the family moving?
2. Why were they moving to Mexico?
3. How long were they planning to stay?
4. How much money did they have?
5. How did they know where to go?
6. How long had God promised to be with them?

OUR FIRST DAY IN MEXICO

Go your ways: behold, I send you forth … Carry
neither purse, nor scrip, nor shoes. Luke 10:3, 4a

The sound of men talking awakened me. Opening my eyes, I
saw two Mexican men speaking with James. Bobby, our five
year old son, stood beside him. Bobby was shivering in the
cold wind. The house was a shack. How glad I was that we
had arrived in the night. At least I'd had a little rest before
laying eyes on my future living quarters.

James came over to the car and said, "I'll go pay the rent
and see if I can get a key for this place."

"Okay," I answered.

Thankfully, the three younger children were still asleep,
so I laid my head back and began praying, *"Oh Lord, please
increase my faith. We have only a few days' food supply."*

It was then I remembered reading the biography of Dwight
L. Moody. His father had died shortly before his mother had
given birth to twins. She was unable to work, so the children
had to hire out for their room and board. Dwight and his
brother cared for a man's cows all winter in exchange for a
place to sleep and only mush to eat. I got the point.

*"Yes, Lord, we have enough corn meal to make mush for
several weeks. Surely you will supply something after that. You*

can do anything. There are plenty of fish in the ocean and wild animals in the hills nearby. Oh yes, and 'the cattle on a thousand hills' are Yours. I'm sure You will give us one whenever our family needs it, won't You, God?" I prayed.

I looked up into the blue sky. Yes! I was serving an awesome God who had control of everything. Looking about me, I saw a field of golden California poppies bobbing their heads as if welcoming me. There were Texas bluebells, sunflowers, and several other flowers that I couldn't name. I could hardly believe the beauty before my eyes. I turned to look in front of the little house. There, across the field, the blue waters of the Pacific Ocean stretched out to the horizon. On either side of our "soon-to-be-home" were several houses, each facing the narrow highway. At least I would have neighbors. *This wasn't the end of the world after all!*

When James returned, he said, "I have good news. The owner said we could just live here and fix up the house for him. He will buy the materials and we will do the work for our rent."

We went inside. "It has a cooking stove!" I shouted, "That's all we need. We have a table, our beds and everything else that's necessary." In shame, I covered my face and cried. God had supplied all we needed.

"Say, I've got a propane tank you can use," said Jose, our new neighbor. "The contract on the tank is *doscientos pesos* (200.00 pesos—about $20.00). By using my tank you will only pay for the propane, which is about $4.50."

We hadn't eaten a decent meal since yesterday morning, so while they went to buy propane, I started hunting through boxes for pans and dishes. That is when I realized I hadn't washed my hands and had been to the outhouse twice. Wipes were not for sale in those days—and there was no water. "Yucky" was hardly the word to describe how I felt!

The children were awake now and Tim and Tricia needed to use the shanty. The smell was horrendous. I gagged while I held each child over the hole. At that moment, I wanted to forget my promise to be a missionary. I wanted to fly back to the States, to a clean bathroom with a toilet that flushed, a lavatory, and a bar of soap.

When I came out of the toilet, I heard a strange, loud noise. Looking around, I saw a boy rolling a fifty-gallon barrel toward me. *"Para el agua,"* (for the water) the boy said, pointing to me. As I pointed to myself, he shook his head, "Yes." I understood. The barrel was for me.

"Look! Look!" I called to the children. "A man driving a bony horse pulling a cart is coming down the road." The boy who had brought the barrel ran out and spoke to him. Then the man pulled right up to our back door where the boy had placed the barrel. He climbed onto his cart, then pouring a bucket of water into my new barrel, he rinsed it out. He then poured bucketful after bucketful of clean water into my barrel. When our barrel was full, the boy gave the man some money. Now we had water! I could wash my hands.

Looking up, I saw two women walking toward me—one had a broom, the other had a mop. Two large boys with hoes over their shoulders and machetes in their hands and three teen-age girls carrying rags were following them. Grass and weeds were two feet tall everywhere, except around the neighbors' houses and driveways. The women explained in sign language that they wanted to help. The boys began cutting away the grass and weeds nearest to the house. The girls and women went inside. They swept down the cobwebs and dust which had collected on the rough board walls. They washed the windows, washed the stove, and mopped the floors of the three small rooms. We looked like busy ants preparing for winter.

The men helped James unload the boxes, our one chest of drawers, and the bunk beds. They screwed the iron legs on the homemade table we had brought. When the work was finished, our wonderful new neighbors bid us good-evening and left. Only the children stayed. The girls took Tricia out into the field. They brought back a beautiful bouquet of wild flowers which we placed on the table.

I sat down on a bed and thanked God for the wonderful new friends who had made my heavy heart light. That night, after seeing God supply a dwelling free of rent, a cook stove, a propane tank, water and friendly, helpful neighbors, my fears of last night seemed far away. I felt a tinge of excitement at the situation. Yes, it was an adventure; but, who doesn't like a little risky venture?

Questions for Discussion:
1. Were the missionaries trusting and obeying God?
2. What beautiful things were around the house?
3. What surprise was inside the house?
4. How did God supply the propane tank?
5. Name some things God supplied that first day?
6. How did the mother's feelings about Mexico change?

No Birthday?

If ye walk in my statutes, and keep my commandments, and do them; I will walk among you, and will be your God, and ye shall be my people. Leviticus 26:3,12

It was Wednesday, March 6, 1962, two weeks after we had moved to Rosarito, Baja California, Mexico.

"Mommy," Bobby said, as he was dressing for bed, "I'll be six years old tomorrow. I can't wait for my birthday. Are things ready for my party?"

All through the day I had been wondering how I would explain to Bobby that there was absolutely no money for a cake or present for his birthday. "Honey, I am very sorry, but we have not been able to get you a present."

"What? Don't stores in Mexico have toys and things?"

"Oh, yes, of course, there are plenty of things to buy, but—but—we have no money right now." He looked so sad. I clenched my jaws to keep from crying.

"Is my birthday going to be worse than this last Christmas? Why can't things be like they were before? We had fun birthdays, picnics at Stony Creek Park and Christmas with everybody. I don't like moving away from everyone: Rada, Cecil, Rudy, and—and—I don't like Mexico." He began sobbing.

I sat down on the bunk bed beside him. I put my arms around him, and he laid his head on my lap. I also remembered those good times in Orland, California. Christmas was like a royal family feast; there were gifts, playing of games, and lots of fun.

Finally, Bobby stopped sobbing and looked up. "You will make me a cake won't you? And can I invite Lalo and Juan?"

I didn't know what to say. I picked up our pillows one at a time and hurled them to the other end of the pallet where James and I slept.

"Why don't you answer me?" Bobby questioned. He dangled his feet, picking up one side of the quilt on our pallet. "You are going to make me a cake, aren't you?"

"I'm sorry Bobby, but I have no sugar, butter, or eggs with which to make a cake. Lie down and I will tell you a story."

"I don't want to hear a story!" He pushed me away.

I slipped out into the kitchen and put on my pajamas, came back and sat down cross-legged on the mattress laying on the floor. I couldn't talk for crying, so we sat in silence. The rain was falling in torrents outside and the cold wind blew into the little room through the cracks around the door and windows. In order to save the scant wood supply, I had let the fire in the heating stove die down. "Come on, get under the cover," I pleaded. He did. Then looking at me he asked, "Are you sure God sent us here?"

"I think He did. Your Daddy fasted and prayed three days before he decided this was the place God wanted us. Things can't always be as we would like them to be. We have food to eat and this place to live out of the cold and rain.

"Remember, God sent a raven each day with food for Elijah. But Elijah also had to suffer. The King's men were hunting Elijah to kill him. That is why he was hiding in the mountains. Elijah may have wished for different food than what the raven brought. We, too, may not always like what God does. But remember, He knows what is best and He will take care of us."

Bobby wiped his eyes and said softly, "Tell me why Daddy wanted to be a missionary." Bobby often said he wanted to be like the Bible character Timothy. In fact, before his brother was born, Bobby had asked that we call him Timothy.

I pulled the cover up around my shoulders and said, "When your father was seventeen years old, during a camp meetings in Myrtle, Missouri, your Grandma encouraged the young people to consecrate their lives to God and go as missionaries. Her friend, Faith Stewart, was a missionary in Cuba, and she needed helpers.

After the camp meeting, they drove to Webb City and stayed a few days with your grandmother's parents, Willie and Effie Hughes. On Labor Day evening they said good-bye to everyone and headed back to California.

About midnight, near Newton, Kansas, a drunk driver raced through a red light and hit them as they pulled out of a gasoline station. The two cars hit head on. Your grandmother, Ella Mae, never regained consciousness. She died in the hospital, twenty minutes later. Your daddy was thrown out of the car. God had already been asking him to dedicate his life for mission work; so while he was sliding down the highway on his chin, he promised God he would be a missionary.

"So Grandma died in a car wreck? What happened to Aunt Esther and Uncle David?"

"Your Uncle David's leg was broken. Your Aunt Esther nor Sister Faith Emily, the woman riding with them, were seriously hurt."

"What else happened?"

"While your father had been driving, he had a feeling that something bad was about to happen. Therefore, he stopped at the gas station and checked the car's engine and tires. They seemed to be fine. Your grandma then took the driver's seat and had just pulled onto the highway when the drunk driver hit them. The girl riding in the other car was thrown through the windshield. When her mother came into the emergency room of the hospital and saw the blood and slashes over her daughter's face, she screamed, 'But honey, I left you asleep in your bedroom!' Bobby, it never pays to disobey your parents."

"Yes, I know, Mama," he replied.

"The girl had climbed out her bedroom window and left with her boyfriend. I'm sure the scars on her face have continually reminded her of her disobedience. Try to go to sleep now," I whispered, and kissed him. "I hear the car, so your Daddy is here."

Questions for Discussion:
1. Who was having a birthday?
2. Why was Bobby crying?
3. Why did his father become a missionary?
4. What happened to the girl who disobeyed?
5. How do you react in difficult situations?

Many times in our darkest moments, Brother Harland Smith would appear bring us comfort, courage, and financial help.

The Birthday Gifts

Be careful for nothing; but in every thing by prayer
and supplication with thanksgiving let your requests
be made known unto God. Philippians 4:6

"Sorry I am so late," James said, "but it took a long time to
get the neighbor's car out of the ditch. This clay ground is like
slime, and yet it sticks like glue. It's like the soil in Southern
Missouri." He slipped off his muddy shoes and his clothes
near the back door where he had entered. He got into his
pajamas and came into the room where I was sitting cross-
legged on our pallet.

"What? Isn't Bobby asleep? Looks like he's been crying?"

"Well, we are feeling pretty sad because there is no money
for his birthday," I answered.

"Why, when is his birthday?"

"It's tomorrow."

"Oh, yes, I know. Well, things could be worse. I was
just visiting with Tomas' sister, Marie. Her baby was crying
because she was hungry and they had no milk."

"You didn't give her the cans of milk in the car?"

"I gave her one of the two cans."

"Rosi drinks a can full every day. What will she do after tomorrow?" I could see myself walking the floor all day and night with Rosi crying for a bottle of milk.

"I'm sorry. I didn't know that was all we had. But I couldn't carry away milk and leave a baby crying of hunger."

"Oh, I know. It's just that I fear what I will do with a hungry baby."

James did all he could to comfort us, but it seemed we had forgotten that Jesus said, "Take therefore no thought for the morrow: for the morrow shall take thought for the things of itself." (Matthew 6:34a)

I covered my head so Bobby couldn't see me crying. I could hear him sniffing until he went to sleep. James wrapped himself in a quilt, and sitting down on the pallet at my feet, he began reading the Bible. I never moved, but I could hear him reading softly. "Blessed is he that considereth the poor: the LORD will deliver him in time of trouble." (Psalms 41:1) "Therefore take no thought, saying, What shall we eat? or, What shall we drink? or, Wherewithal shall we be clothed? (For after all these things do the Gentiles seek:) for your heavenly Father knoweth that ye have need of all these things. But seek ye first the kingdom of God, and his righteousness; and all these things shall be added unto you. Take therefore no thought for the morrow: for the morrow shall take thought for the things of itself. Sufficient unto the day is the evil thereof." (Matthew 6:31-34)

He prayed quietly for a while and then got under the covers. Soon, he was snoring heavily.

I pretended to be asleep. I was thinking, *wondering how he thought we might get milk for Rosi? I knew cans of milk wouldn't be falling out of the sky like the manna in the wilderness. During his growing up years, his father, a minister, sometimes traveled as an evangelist. That had given him firsthand experience seeing how God met their needs. I suppose these experiences were like foundation stones in a building. They made his faith steady for times like this. I had grown up on a farm in Oregon. Our necessities were bought with hard-earned money. We always had plenty of food. In the summer and fall we stored away enough food to last until the coming harvest. I was very uncomfortable having only enough food for a few weeks, much less for only one day! I tossed and turned on the hard floor until I finally fell into a restless sleep.*

Sometime later, we were awakened by loud knocking on the front door. "Jaime! Jaime!" Someone was shouting.

"*¿Quién es?*" (Who is it?) James muttered half asleep.

"*Yo soy Jose.* (I am Jose) *Aquí está Smit. Smit.*" The voice answered.

"It must be Bro. Smith," I said.

"Ah, you're dreaming," James responded.

But, he realized it was true when he heard the familiar voice of Brother Harland Smith. He jumped up, jerked the door open, and shouted, "Get in here out of the rain!"

"It is pretty wet out there, and this house doesn't have a porch," Bro. Smith said as the two men stepped inside. Then in his usual polite way he added, "I hated to come in on you so late, but I started as soon as I got off work. It rained hard all the way, so I couldn't drive very fast. How is everyone?"

"We are all right, but how did you find us?" James asked.

"I really didn't know where to start—with no address, or phone. When we came through last weekend, I asked around, but no one knew of an American family in town. However, all day while at work, I kept thinking I must come and find you. The longer I worked, the more convinced I was that I must come tonight. I prayed all the way for God to help me. Back up the road a short distance, I saw a man bent over struggling to stay afoot in this awful storm. I stopped and offered him a ride. We talked just a little, and then I realized he was the man you had brought to Pomona when you came to get more of your things. Of course he guided me right here."

"Thanks, Jose," James said as he shook his hand. Jose said good night and left.

"It was a real miracle that the timing was just right for you to meet Jose," James said.

"Yes, God does all things well. We just have to listen and follow him," Bro. Smith said, as he handed some letters to James. "There are more boxes in the pickup. I'll get them in the morning."

The minute I heard Bro. Smith's voice, I knew God had not forsaken us. He had sent help. If there are living angels, Harland Smith was one. His face had a radiance which gave the impression of being divine. In his presence, burdens vanished; fear and discouragement lost their control. There was an influence going out from him that changed the hearts of those with whom he talked. It inspired them to have a determination to go on for God, no matter the cost. I had many times felt heavenly power when he prayed. *But why had I been so discouraged a few hours ago?* "Oh, God, please forgive me!" I prayed.

Before the children awoke, the men had unloaded the boxes. There were two packages for Bobby. One was from Rada, a friend who called Bobby her grandson, another one was from Mary Ellen, a girl who had lived with us. The last box was full of groceries. It contained cans of evaporated milk (for Rosi), a box of cake mix, eggs, and confectioners sugar for frosting.

I lay the beautifully wrapped presents on the bed beside Bobby. Then I bent over, kissed him and said, "Wake-up, Bobby! It's your birthday! Go invite Lalo and Juan to share the birthday cake I'm making for you."

Questions for Discussion:
 1. What has God promised for those who help the poor?
 2. Why did James give away the milk?
 3. How did Brother Smith find their house?
 4. Why did he drive through the storm to come to them?
 5. What did he bring?

Church Service in Rosarito Beach

I was glad when they said unto me, Let us go
into the house of the LORD. Psalms 122:1

I heard a gentle tap-tap-tapping on the door one Saturday morning. *"¿Quién es?"* (Who is it?) James asked, as he opened the door.

I looked up from the book I was reading and saw Jose standing there.

"Pásale," (Come in) James said, and motioned with his hand for Jose to enter.

"Don't need to come in," he said, "I just wanted to know what you will be doing tomorrow. Are you going to invite people again to come, sing, and listen to your talk?"

"That is what we plan to do. We came here to tell the story of Jesus," James replied. "Say, could you understand my Spanish last Sunday?"

"Yes, sure, at least part of what you said. I liked the singing mostly, and I really liked that one about the cross."

"I'm so glad. Do come over in the morning, and we'll sing it again."

"Okay, I will, and I'll be going now. *Hasta Mañana!"* (See you tomorrow!).

"See you tomorrow," James said as he closed the door.

I laid down the Bible story book which I had been reading to the children and picked up the print-outs of a few Spanish songs. "Let's see, he must have meant 'En La Cruz.' Now what page is it?" I asked, as I shuffled the papers in my hands.

"Maybe he meant the one about a cross on the mountain," Bobby said. "Remember, you told me it said that."

"I don't think we sang that one well enough for anyone to understand the words," I remarked with a smile. "That one is really hard to sing."

"Me sing," Tricia said. "Me sing," and she started jabbering in high and low tones, trying to mimic the Spanish she was hearing everyday.

"No playing right now," I cautioned. "We are worshiping God. How about singing 'Jesus Loves Me'?"

"After we finish singing in English, we'll try learning it in Spanish," James suggested.

"That's a good idea, and then let's sing, 'En La Cruz' and some other songs to practice up for tomorrow," I said.

"After that, I need to study my Spanish. Maybe I can make myself better understood," James said.

"I think you did pretty well. The people were giving their full attention to you, James. Now let's sing: 'Jesus loves me,'" I said.

Bob & Tricia
singing in worship

Jesus loves me! this I know,
For the Bible tells me so;
Little ones to him belong,
They are weak but He is strong.

Yes, Jesus loves me!
Yes, Jesus loves me!
Yes, Jesus loves me!
The Bible tells me so.

Then we sang:

Cristo me ama!
Cristo me ama!
Cristo me ama!
La Biblia dice así…

There in our living area that also served as a bedroom, the children fell asleep while James and I continued practicing

Spanish hymns. The lower half of a bunk bed was pushed against the north wall and the upper half was against the south wall. These beds also served as two sofas, so while sitting on their beds for worship, they lay down and went to sleep.

It was a cozy little house, and the children never fussed about going to bed because we were all together. I tucked each one in and kissed the sleeping little darlings. Then, I said good night to James, who was staying up to study Spanish.

James and I slept on a mattress in the kitchen area except when it was storming. During a storm, the rain blew in through the cracks in the walls. On those nights, we carried our mattress into the living room where there was just enough room for it to fit perfectly on the floor between the bunk beds.

Tonight the weather was calm. I lowered the mattress from where it leaned against the wall during the day and made up the bed with the sheets and a blanket from the cardboard box in the corner. Soon, I fell asleep to the rhythm of James repeating, *"Cristo manifestado en la carne." "Cristo, el hijo de Dios, manifestado en la carne."*

The following day was sunny and warm. Soon, after we had finished breakfast, Pedro Sanchez, his wife, and some children arrived. He introduced his wife, Beatrice, and shook hands with James, me, and our two older children. "We came for the church service. You are having one, aren't you?"

"That is right. A few can sit here," James said, pointing to the beds. "The others will have to stand. We don't have chairs or benches like a church does."

"Oh, that's all right," he said.

I motioned for them to come in and sit down. Beatrice came in and told the children to greet us. In the Mexican traditional manner, each child respectfully shook hands with James, me, and our children, saying to each of us, *"Dios le bendiga,"* (God bless you). They then sat down quietly beside Beatrice. I was amazed at their politeness. *I think I'm going to love the Mexican culture,* I thought.

As a child, I had been taught to shake hands when greeting people and to show extra respect to the adults by putting a title before their names, just as these children had done. We were also required to answer, "Yes, Sir," or "Yes, Madam." We had to sit quietly and were not allowed to intrude into adult conversations. However, there was no danger of these children interrupting our conversation since I couldn't speak Spanish and Beatrice couldn't speak English. We just looked at each other and smiled.

Soon, Jose, his dad, his mother, and his sister came in. Later Cipriana came with her little boy, who was the same age as Rosi. She had moved into a house behind ours the week after we came. She and I were both homesick, so we became good friends quickly. We used pictures and sign language to illustrate our conversations.

James passed out the leaflet of songs and motioned for everyone to stand. He then bowed his head and said a short prayer he had memorized. After that, he said, *"Número cinco* (number five). When everyone had found the song we sang:

> *En la cruz, en la cruz*
> *do primero vi la luz*
> *Y las manchas de*
> *mi alma yo lavé. . . ."*

I was surprised how good it sounded.

Standing in the crowd gathered at the door, I noticed a young man with his head lifted to the sky. Tears were streaming down his cheeks. I kept my eyes on him while James read a few scriptures from the Bible and talked. The man seemed so interested, as if he had been very thirsty and was enjoying a good drink of fresh cool water.

When the service was over, the man said to James, "I am Tomas Mendoza. Pedro is my brother. Pedro has been to the United States, and while there he heard about Christ. He persuaded me to go with him to the Baptist church. There I heard that Jesus died to take away my sins, that I could believe in Him, and be saved. I accepted the message, now Jesus is my Savior. The words you read are so beautiful. I wish I had a book like that."

"I'll see if I can get one for you," James promised.

The children played tag for a while, and then the people left. Our second teaching service in Spanish was history.

"It wasn't as hard as I had thought it would be," James said.

"The people seemed to like it, especially Tomas. And the singing sounded pretty good."

"I sing too," Tricia said, and started singing words that we couldn't understand. Tim joined her. They seemed to understand each other although James and I could only understand "Cristo."

Questions for Discussion:
1. Did Jose want to come to the church service?
2. Which song did he like best?
3. Why had James moved the family to Rosarito?
4. Did Tomas Mendoza seem to love God?
5. Who wanted a Bible?
6. Why is it important to attend church?

THE BROKEN CLOTHESLINE

*Be ye angry, and sin not: let not the sun go
down upon your wrath: Ephesians 4:26*

April 1962—Everyday was laundry day in Baja. James rigged
up a clothesline for me and every day I filled it with diapers,
underwear, little dresses, shirts, and pants.

It was THE JOB I quickly learned to hate. I had loved
washdays when I was a child. At a very young age, my family
lived in Oklahoma City. We had electricity, running water,
and used a washing machine.

We moved to Oregon when I was eight years old. There
we lived for two years in an old settler's house that had no
electricity; it was like going back in time. We had to pump
water from a well by hand. We sorted our clothes on Friday
evening and soaked them overnight in soapy water to be ready
for Saturday, our wash day. Then each piece of clothing was
hand washed using a scrub board. All day Saturday we took
turns scrubbing and rinsing the clothes. In warm weather,
when Mama wasn't watching, we had lots of fun playing in
the water on wash day.

The situation was different now. The scrubbing, rinsing,
wringing, and hanging on the line were my daily responsibility
and mine alone. Mom and my two older sisters weren't there

to share the load. Why didn't I hire someone to do it? There were two reasons: 1. We didn't have enough money. 2. We wanted to live on the same level as those we were ministering to. *(Jesus came to the earth and lived like we humans do. It was said of Jesus that *he was tempted in all points as we are tempted, yet without sin.)* James and I both thought we should experience what our neighbors experienced so we could better comprehend the way they thought about life. It did help because before long, we were thinking and talking like them; even though learning the culture and language this way wasn't easy.

Having always used an automatic washing machine to do our laundry, my hands were soft and delicate. After a week of washing our clothes, my hands became severely inflamed. However, there was no quitting just because blisters were all along my index fingers and thumbs. The blisters on the outside of my knuckles were broken and sometimes bled. Just the same, *cloth diapers* for two babies had to be washed every day. Always afterwards, when I saw a line full of clothes hanging out to dry, I would feel sorry for the person who had washed them.

After we had lived there for several weeks and my hands had healed, I decided to try washing our bed sheets. After that huge job was finished and I looked at the white sheets hanging on the line blowing in the sea breeze, I felt like I had climbed a mountain and that I was standing on top with my hands raised, shouting victory! I was tired, so I gave the children a snack lunch, and we all fell asleep together.

An hour or so later, James came home and awakened me with sad news. "The clothesline has broken and the sheets were dragging on the ground," he said.

I sat up and held my head in my hands. "It took all morning to wash those sheets," I groaned.

"I'm so sorry," James said. "I'll help you rewash them."

"Thanks," I said with sarcasm. Trying hard to stay in control, I said, "James, why can't you repair that clothesline so this won't happen again? This is the third time it has broken, and I've had to wash the clothes the second time. It's not easy to wash clothes." My back and arms ached, my hands hurt, and inside I was feeling somewhat like a two year old on the floor kicking and screaming. I lay back on the mattress. Satan and his imps were whispering. *You are so mistreated. You can't take anymore. You might as well give up and go home. James doesn't care about you. He's got his mind on his goals for winning people and doesn't care how much you suffer for his calling to be a missionary.* Trying to shut out the nagging of my mind, I covered my eyes.

"Come on, I'll help you," James said, extending his hand to help me get up.

"You would say that when there is no water," I retorted. "We can't wash now. By the time the water man comes tomorrow, the dirt will be dried on the sheets, and they will be twice as hard to wash." I wanted to cry, to run away from it all.

James was already outside when I murmured, "I wish things could be different." I could hear him whistling as he banged the wash tubs around. Being curious about what he was doing, I went out to see. He was working on the clothes line. He had brought the dirty sheets from off the ground and put them in the rinse water that I had left. Then he had covered them with an empty tub.

I lifted the empty tub and peeked in. Straw was floating on the dirty water. The sheets I had soaked in Clorox and hung out 'white as snow' were horrid. They had not only fallen onto the dirt, but the wind had dragged them back and forth, back and forth, sweeping the ground. A big portion of the sheets were stained dirt brown. "I guess we will have beige colored sheets from now on," I grumbled. "I wish I could keep them white like my mother did," I fussed, as I remembered how careful she was about white clothes staying white. We had to scrub, soak, and sometimes we boiled them. She would place a big boiler tub full of water on the wood cook stove, and we would fire up the stove. Then she would put the white clothes into the tub and boil the clothes the way we did meat and vegetables. They came out sparkling white.

"My problem is not the way I wash," I fumed. "It is James and the clothes line." The remainder of the afternoon I raged war in my mind while trying to be a sweet mother.

Rosi was crying again, so I picked her up. What was my real problem? My problem was anger. I knew the Bible said, *Be ye angry, and sin not. Can a person be angry and not sin?* I pondered, as I changed Rosi's diaper.

"What is bothering you?" Bobby asked. I could see him standing in the doorway a frown on his face. "I called you three times! Tim fell down in the mud. I tried to keep him out of it and almost fell down myself."

I saw Tim waddling toward the house with his arms stretched out. He was crying and mud was dripping from his arms. "Looks like you wallowed in the puddle," I said.

Just then I heard, *"Agua, agua,"* (water).

"Oh, look Mama, a new water man," Bobby shouted as he pointed to an old pickup with four water barrels in its bed.

"Wonderful!" I shouted. "Run and wave him down."

I put Rosi's snow pants back on her, got a quarter out of my purse, and gave it to Bobby who had come back for money to pay the man. "Here, Tricia, you'll have to take care of Rosi while I dress Tim and rewash the sheets. Keep her in the house out of this wind. Her fever just cleared up yesterday. She will be okay on the floor. She has on her heavy clothes."

To keep the mud out of the house, I stripped Tim outside. Then I wrapped my sweater around his shivering body and carried him inside. "Ugh! More washing," I sighed while putting clean clothes on him. "Now, stay in here and play with Rosi. Tricia, watch him closely and don't let him out. Here, I'll lock the door."

By now it was after 5:00 p.m. James had already gone out to the Tomato Ranch where Tomas and Pedro worked. He met them every day after work for a time of prayer and reading the Bible, as neither of them had a Bible.

Bobby helped me fill a tub with water and I salvaged the sheets from the dirty water. While I worked, I was raging war with Satan. He had me down and was clawing away at me.

The sheets were ready to hang before dark. "Let's hang them in the morning, so we can keep an eye on them until they are dry," I said as I covered the tub full of my white sheets, turned beige.

When James came home, I had him bring the tub full of sheets into the house to keep them safe during the night. "Wow! No wonder the clothes line broke," he said. "Wet sheets are heavy."

"I know," I said. "I've handled them all day. Well, not quite all day."

During family worship that night, I asked James, "Isn't there a verse that says to put away all anger?"

He looked in his Bible concordance, then said, "It's in Ephesians 4:31."

I found it and read, "'Let all bitterness, and wrath, and anger, and clamor, and evil speaking, be put away from you. . .' And here is the one I've been thinking of all day, 'Be ye angry, and sin not: let not the sun go down upon your wrath.' That's the verse Mama used to quote to us when we would fight. My older sister, Lois, was always first to apologize for getting angry during the day. Then we would each apologize."

My prayer that night was: "Oh, Lord, forgive me for being angry. Cleanse me from bitter thoughts against James. Teach me how to resist thoughts from Satan. I don't want thoughts to harbor in my mind until they turn my heart bitter."

Questions for Discussion:
1. Why did the mother hate to do laundry?
2. Why had she become angry?
3. What verse came to her mind?
4. Can a person be angry and not sin?
5. What should a person do with anger?

Edith Cole came to visit three years after "The Broken Clothesline" story. She is helping us with that day's laundry.

NO TELEPHONE

God is our refuge and strength,
a very present help in trouble. Psalms 46:1

May 1962. "Mama, Mama! Something is wrong with Rosi.
She won't get up," Tricia screamed. I threw down the dish
cloth and rushed outside. Rosi lay sprawled on the beach-
pebbled walkway by the back door.

"Oh, no," I cried as I bent over to pick her up. "She is as
limp as a rag doll," I gasped. I laid her on my shoulder and
patted her gently, whispering in her ear, "Rosi, Rosi, wake up.
Rosi, wake-up!" She didn't respond. I shook her lightly being
careful not to bounce her head around. She didn't respond. I
shook her harder! I laid her on the bed and started to breathe
into her mouth, but she was breathing on her own.

Falling on my knees, I invoked God as earnestly as I
could, saying, "God, please don't take my baby, please, God,
please." Bobby and Tricia fell on their knees beside me. Two-
year-old Tim sensed the urgency of our prayers. He leaned
against me, saying repeatedly, "Jesus, Jesus, Jesus."

I felt so alone, so frightened. Where was anyone to help
me? James was away visiting, we had no telephone, and no
praying neighbors. There was no one near who understood my
language. Until then, I had not realized how much I depended

on others' prayers. Whenever I needed God's attention, I would call someone on the phone to agree with me in prayer for the situation. Of course, my first thoughts were always to call James if he was there to pray. (He almost always got his prayers answered.) Every time after James finished praying for the children, they seemed to feel better. If it was night they would go to sleep again. Sometimes when I thought he wasn't awake enough to know what he was praying about, God understood and answered his prayers. Today he was not home. As far as I knew, the nearest phone (where I might call someone I knew) was downtown, three miles away.

I had to depend on God alone. I shook Rosi again. I washed her face in cold water. I prayed as I walked the floor bouncing her around trying to get her back to consciousness. A hundred thoughts ran through my mind. *If Rosi died what would happen? How could we get her body back across the international border without a doctor's signed death certificate? What doctor would believe that she just fell over dead? I feared that people would think God's curse, instead of his blessing, was on us.* "Lord, please help us," I cried again.

All of us except Rosi had adjusted to the change from living in a house that stayed at 70° temperature day and night into living in this house that might change from a cool 45° to a hot 85° on any given day. (It would get very hot when we built a fire in the wood heating stove.)

Rosi was ten months old at this time and not very healthy. She was born with a heart murmur and hadn't gotten off to a strong start in life. During her first seven weeks she could not breathe when lying on her back. At seven weeks of age, our church had a special day of fasting and prayer for her healing. Praise God! A few days afterward, a heart specialist told us her heart was working almost normal and that she should be all right.

Thank the Lord, from that time on, she had no problems with her heart. We were confident that God had healed her. However, the last two months since coming to Baja, she had been sick most of the time with fever, chest congestion, coughing, runny nose and matted eyes. I felt like it was because our house was so cold most of the time and she had to be almost stripped to change her diaper. When using cloth diapers, a child has to be changed many times a day. If they are not changed often, they may develop a diaper rash; also, their clothes and bedding would get wet which would add to the dangers of the cold. I questioned if the two months of this sickness had weakened her heart. Did that cause the unconsciousness? Now that Rosi was big enough to walk, Tricia sometimes took her outside into the warm sunshine. She must have slipped or tripped on a rock when she fell. But why would such a little fall cause her to pass out?

I was still walking, shaking, and praying. "Is she dying?" Tricia questioned, as she wiped the tears from her cheeks with the back of her hand.

Bobby was standing beside me wholly composed and confident. I caught his eyes. They signaled to me, "She'll be all right, Mama."

Suddenly, Rosi raised her head, leaned back in my arms, and looked at me with a puzzled expression on her face. Tricia and Bobby held out their hands for her to come to them. She shook her head "no" and laid it back on my shoulder. How wonderful her movements felt! "Thank you, Lord!" I cried and burst into uncontrollable sobbing.

"What's wrong? Why you crying?" Tricia asked.

"Because I'm happy! See, Rosi is alive and well!!"

"Rm, r-r-mm, r-r-mm," Tim was saying. I knew he was hearing his daddy's motorcycle. Bobby ran out to meet James, hoping (I thought) that James would take him for a short ride.

Tim toddled behind Bobby. Tricia covered her ears with her hands. She and I both hated motorcycle noises.

Bobby jumped on behind James, while James placed Timmy in front of him; then he spun back out of the driveway and onto the highway. In just a few minutes they came back beaming, like boys do when they go fast. "Tomorrow I'll take you with me, and we will go to the ranch on the other side of that hill," James was telling Bobby as they came inside.

"Do be careful," I said. "We don't need another scare. I've just gotten over one."

"Why? What happened that scared you?" asked James.

"Rosi almost died," Tricia said.

"What?" James questioned.

"Tricia was playing outside with her. Rosi must have slipped on the beach pebbles by the back door. When I picked her up, she was unconscious. She was limp as a rag, and it seemed like forever before she was again conscious," I answered.

"You don't think she fainted and then fell?" James asked, as he reached down and picked her up. "I'm so glad you are okay. God took care of you, didn't He?" James said.

"Yes, but it sure was frightening!" I added.

Questions for Discussions:
1. What happened to Rosi?
2. Who had been sick for two months?
3. Was God hearing them when they prayed?
4. Who was their refuge?
5. Who was taking care of the family?

The Motorcycle Accident

In thee, O LORD, do I put my trust: let me
never be put to confusion. Deliver me in thy
righteousness, and cause me to escape: incline
thine ear unto me, and save me. Psalms 71:1, 2

"Rm, r-r-mm, r-r-mm," Tim was saying. He could hear his
daddy's motorcycle. Bobby ran out to meet James, hoping
to get a ride as he usually did. Tim toddled behind Bobby.
Tricia covered her ears with her hands. Suddenly, a dog began
howling like a car had hit it. I wondered what had happened.

"Mama, Mama, come quick, it's Daddy!" I heard Bobby
yelling.

I turned off the stove, pulled the rice off the burner, picked
up Rosi and hurried out the door. Tricia trailed after me.
Bobby was running along the edge of the highway.

By the time I got to where I could see James, he was sitting
up in the middle of the highway holding his head in his hands.
I looked both ways to see if a car might be approaching. All
was clear. I saw his motorcycle laying mashed up against the
post in front of the small rodeo arena that was a little south
and across the highway from our house. I saw James roll over,
then get up and dust off his pants. He staggered toward the
side of the road. I saw blood on his shirt and face.

"Are you hurt?" I asked. I felt frightened, hot and weak.

"Not much, just my chin and shoulder," he said. He rubbed his shoulder and was trying to move it.

"Blood is dripping off your face," Bobby shouted, "and there is a big gash in your chin."

By now several neighbors were running toward us. Jose picked up Tim who was toddling behind us. Concha took Tricia's hand and tried to comfort her. I was thankful for our neighbors. I felt their sympathy.

James took his handkerchief from his pocket and held it on his chin to stop the bleeding. "What happened?" I asked. "I heard a dog howling."

"I hit that dog," James said pointing to a dog dragging himself across the field. "There were two dogs fighting in the road. I honked and they scattered, one on each side of the road. Then, that one dashed back across the road right in front of me. I must have broken its back. Do you know the owner?" James asked Jose's father.

"I think it is a stray. I haven't seen it around here," he replied.

"That's good! At least no neighbor will be angry with me." We had already learned that our neighbors valued their dogs. They trusted their dogs for protection.

"I'm glad it didn't kill you. It could have," I said.

"Yes, it could have. I was going pretty fast. I flew straight out in front of the motorcycle, landed on my chin, and slid a long way down the highway. I suppose the impact could have broken my neck if I had hit differently; it could have killed me, or maybe left me paralyzed."

We headed back to the house, James limping along holding his hankie on his chin. "You must have hurt your leg," I remarked.

Jose had seen the motorcycle and went to get it. The fender was bent back against the tire holding it still. After some prying and bending he was able to get the tire free to roll. He pushed it over beside our house. James patted his bright red motorcycle as we passed by it. "I guess you will get some rest for a while. You've been a good pack mule," he said.

I poured clean drinking water into a bowl and washed James' chin. Then I taped on a clean bit of gauze. While the bleeding was subsiding, James cut a butterfly bandage and I taped the gash closed.

Later, while James was sipping some soup and the children were eating rice for supper, I asked, "Did you get to check on the baby that was sick yesterday?"

"Yes, I did. The sores were completely gone. Her mother showed me. The inside of her mouth was smooth and clean."

"Oh, that is great," I said. "I felt so sorry for that baby. With all those sores she couldn't suck and would certainly get worse without being able to take nourishment."

"Yes, God is good."

"And, He is good 'cause he kept you from getting your neck broken," Bobby added.

Questions for Discussion:
1. Why did Timmy and Bobby run to their father?
2. What happened to James?
3. Why did James ask about the dog's owner?
4. What had James been doing?
5. Who healed the baby?
6. Who protected James from worse injuries?

Fun at the Beach

I have been young, and now am old; yet
have I not seen the righteous forsaken, nor
his seed begging bread. Psalms 37:25

It was June, 1962. We were still living in the tiny house just
outside of Rosarito Beach, Baja California, Mexico. It was
near the Pacific Ocean, so fog usually hid the sun until 9 a.m.
each morning. Today was different. I had been up for a while
and the sun was bright and warm, so I called to the sleeping
children, "Get up and we'll go to the beach."

Bobby yawned and opened one eye. "Are we going to the
beach?" he asked.

Mary Ellen stretched her long arms over her head and
swung her big feet out onto the rough, wood floor. "Great
idea!" she said.

"Yea, let's go," Rudy answered. "Maybe we can catch a
fish. I'd like fish for supper."

"Okay, as soon as we eat our breakfast and get our morning
work done," I told them.

Besides our four small children, three teenagers were staying
with us. Shirley Stice normally helped missionaries Edith
Cole and Ruby Marken on the Pai Pai Indian Reservation
in Santa Catarina. Since Edith and Ruby had gone to their

respective homes for the summer, Shirley had come to stay with us. Mary Ellen and her brother, Rudy, had also come to stay a month with us while school was out in California. This made nine living in our tiny house.

Mary Ellen had lived with us in Orland, California since before Tim was born. She helped care for our children, so she felt right at home getting them dressed and ready. She filled two baby bottles of milk for Rosi—one for her mid-morning feeding and one to carry to the beach. Then she filled bowls with hot oatmeal (without milk) for Rosi, Tim and herself. Tim loved oats, with milk or without, but the instant he had satisfied his hunger, the bowl with the remaining oats went on his head for a hat! Any oats left in the bowl stuck on his hair or dripped down his face onto his clothes. Mary knew Tim's tricks, so she kept an eye on him as she was feeding Rosi and getting a few bites from her own bowl.

Rudy and Bobby rolled up the sleeping bags. Then they picked up the mattress that James and I slept on and leaned it against the wall. "Shall we fill the two laundry tubs with water from the water barrel outside?" Rudy asked.

"Yes," I answered. "We need to wash a few clothes and hang them out to dry before we leave." Washing was a back-breaking job, and if we didn't wash everyday, it was almost impossible to have clean clothes. Besides that, we had only one clothesline on which to dry the wet clothes. It would only hold laundry for one day.

Shirley and Tricia put away toys and clothes and then Shirley swept the floors.

James had already gone to help Tomas Mendoza build himself a shack at the tomato ranch where Tomas was working. Tomas had committed his life to Christ a few weeks before we had moved to Rosarito. Since he had met James, the two were knit together like the Bible characters David and Jonathan.

They prayed, studied the Bible, visited the sick and did other things together almost every day.

When the tubs were filled, the girls went out to wash clothes while Rudy and Bobby sat down to eat.

"I don't want oats," Bobby complained. "We have oats every day."

"How about some fried potatoes?" I asked.

"No, we have potatoes every day, too," he answered.

"Sorry, that is all we have," I said.

"I'm so tired of oats, potatoes, and split beans. Can't we have something else?" He hung his head over the bowl of oats that I had set before him, wrinkled his nose, and then looked up at me. There was such a pitiful look on his face. That's when I noticed the dark circles under his eyes. Our diet was taking a toll on him. I knew he was hungry; but he needed something a little more appetizing. I felt so bad, I wanted to cry. Bobby was so obedient and so careful about serving God. I wondered if the tests of faith which we were having would ruin his love for Christ.

"We'll have fish for supper," Rudy said cheerfully.

"Yes, Bobby, don't you remember on your birthday how God sent gifts?" I added.

"Then let's go and catch the biggest fish in the world. Can Rudy and I go ahead?"

"We'd better stay together. Go help the girls finish the washing while I clean up these dishes."

We finished washing, rinsing and hanging out the clothes. Now with dresses, shirts, pants, pajamas and diapers on the line to dry, we started out across the field toward the beach. Bobby and Rudy, with Tim on his shoulders, led the way. The tall grass that had covered the field in Feburary when we had moved here was dry. The boys tramping ahead made a path for us. Mary carried Rosi; I held Tricia by the hand and carried a bag of towels and other things we might need. Tricia was afraid there were bugs or snakes in the tall grass, so she held me tight and complained about the dry grass scratching her legs. However, she forgot about snakes and bugs whenever she saw a pretty flower and wanted to run aside and pick it.

The water reflected the beautiful bright blue sky. It stretched out before us as far as we could see. I closed my eyes and listened to the seagulls calling while I inhaled the fresh ocean breeze. *Oh, God,* I said in my heart, *You have created this. You can do anything. How could I ever doubt that you will provide. When will I realize that this present lack of tasty food is only a lesson for me? Increase my faith.* I kicked off my shoes and wiggled my toes down into the warm sand. It felt so-o-o good. The children and teenagers had already shed their shoes and were racing to the water. "Watch out for Tim!" I called when I saw him toddling behind them near the water's edge. "The waves will knock him down."

Mary raced for Tim just as a wave toppled him. Holding Rosi in one arm, she grabbed him with the other just as he fell. He screamed and she carried him back to me. I cuddled his cold, shuddering body. "Me no like," he said, "bad, bad, wata no good." (It was at least a year before Tim would again wade into the ocean.)

Mary spread out the blanket and sat Rosi on it. Then she ran to hunt for shells with Shirley and Tricia. Tim was soon building roads in the sand and driving shell cars over them. It was time for Rosi's morning nap, so I moved her and her blanket under a bush to shade her from the sun and she went to sleep. With Rosi asleep and Tim playing contentedly, I relaxed and talked to the Lord.

Questions for Discussion:
1. What was unusual about this morning?
2. What jobs did the children do?

3. Did each one help with the work?
4. Should parents teach their children to work?
5. Do you help at your house?
6. Did they have fun at the beach?

Fish for Supper

For this cause I bow my knees unto the Father of our
Lord Jesus Christ . . . [who] is able to do exceeding
abundantly above all that we ask or think, according
to the power that worketh in us. Ephesians 3:14, 20

Rudy and Bobby were playing in the water and Tim in the
sand. Mary, Shirley, and Tricia were still gathering shells.
With Rosi sleeping in the shade, I took the time to meditate
and talk to God.

"God," I said, "you know I am embarrassed to serve split
beans, potatoes and oats to my American guests every day.
It has been a long time since we've had a salad. That would
be such a treat! You created everything in this world, so how
about creating some better food for us? I don't want these
young folks to believe this is the way you always treat your
workers. Aren't we worth more than this? My children want a
gallon of cold milk delivered to their home each day as it was
before we became missionaries. And I would like some fruit
for them and . . ." When I had finally finished complaining,
I waited for an answer. God was silent. He caused me to
remember Bobby's birthday. In foolish despair I had cried
myself to sleep when food and gifts were already on their
way. God had already sent Bro. Smith with all we needed;

however, because of the storm, he had not arrived at our house until late that night. I felt a sting of reproof and repented for complaining. Afterwards a warm pleasant feeling came over me and I began singing Frederick M. Lehman's song.

The Love of God
Could we with ink the ocean fill,
And were the skies of parchment made;
Were every stalk on earth a quill,
And every man a scribe by trade;

To write the love of God above
Would drain the ocean dry;
Nor could the scroll contain the whole,
Though stretched from sky to sky.

Oh, love of God, how rich and pure!
How measureless and strong!
It shall forever more endure—
The saints' and angels' song.

I sang it over again, and again, and again. I wrote in big letters in the sand, God is Love. I felt God's big arms around me. "I'm sorry God, for doubting your love. I know you have a plan that I don't see," I said as I was writing in the sand.

Earlier the children had built homes, ranches and castles in the sand. *These will be destroyed by the rising tide,* I thought. *And so it is with the homes, enterprises, bank accounts, and any other thing we have upon this earth; they will all be destroyed before long by fire. God has told us in His Word. "The earth also and the works that are therein shall be burned up."* (2 Peter 3:10)

After a while, Mary, Shirley and Tricia came back with their arms full of shells. We talked about how God had provided a shell home that was just right for the different animals. As we were talking, I was reminded of the portion of scripture that tells us how God cares for the birds and the grass of the field; also that we are of much more value than them and He will always care for us. We talked about the vastness of the ocean and about the expanse of blue sky overhead. It was awesome! Mary began singing.

When through the woods and forest glades I wander
And hear the birds sing sweetly in the trees;
When I look down from lofty mountains grandeur
And hear the brook and feel the gentle breeze:

Then sings my soul, My Savior God, to thee,
HOW GREAT THOU ART! HOW GREAT THOU ART!
Then sings my soul, My Savior God to thee:
HOW GREAT THOU ART! HOW GREAT THOU ART!
(Stuart K. Hine)

Then Rudy and Bobby, tired of playing in the water, came and joined us. We sang again all the verses that we could remember.

"I wish I had a fishing pole. I could catch a fish for supper," Rudy said.

"Me, too," Bobby agreed. "We all want to fish."

"Let's dig clams," I suggested. We did, but we had only our hands with which to dig; therefore, all we dug up were little sand diggers.

I supposed that the children were getting hungry by now, so I suggested we go home to eat. They quickly vetoed my suggestion and continued playing for several more hours.

When the sun was getting close to the horizon, I called, "We had better start for home. You are wet and will get very cold as soon as the sun is down." As I was gathering up the few things we had brought, a car drove up.

I had often wondered how I could protect myself and all my small children. I would not run and leave them unprotected; however, today there was no need of fear. I was not alone. Besides, the car was quite a distance from us. I thought no more about it until I looked up again and saw two men walking toward us. They were carrying a fish! The boys saw it too and came running.

"There's our fish," they shouted as they ran toward me.

"Sell fish to you," the man said. "No sell today. Day late, must sell. For you, just two dollars."

I was quivering with anticipation. My legs felt like they would buckle under me, and my jaws were trembling. In my limited Spanish I tried to say, "I would love to have that fish, but I don't have two dollars." The man displayed anger as if he thought I was lying to him.

Then Shirley, who knew a lot of Spanish words, told him what I had tried to say. He became very angry; he shouted some words in Spanish that neither Shirley nor I could understand and started walking away. My heart beat fast. Thoughts of frying up that fish for supper flashed through my mind. I prayed: *Lord, please don't disappoint us, here is a good time for you to show us that your love is greater than the amount of water in this ocean.*

The two men walked away; then, as suddenly as he had turned away, the leader turned around and walked back to us. "I'll give fish for money you have in pocket." He pointed to me and pulled his pockets inside out.

I got his point. We were all standing together by this time and were looking wishfully at the big fish. I held out my hand and said, "The man says he'll trade the fish for the money we have. Let's see how much we can collect." We all dug in our pockets. The boys turned theirs inside out. All together, Mary, Shirley and Rudy had seventeen cents. I had not a penny. The man became even more angry and shouted again. This time my heart skipped a beat. I thought for sure he was going away with his fish.

God softened his heart and he said, "I take money. You take big fish." He placed the fish carefully in my two outstretched arms and gave a little bow as if he was giving me a gift. Truly, it was a gift, for seventeen cents would not have paid for its head. (Fish heads are sold in fish markets here to be used for making fish head soup which is a delicious soup.)

I held the fish beside six-year-old Bobby. It was the length that he was tall. We took turns carrying it home.

I didn't know much about cleaning fish, but I did the best I could. We cut it in pieces. I sent the children with portions to our three neighbors. After we had eaten all we wanted, we rubbed salt into the remaining fish to preserve it.

That night many families thanked God that they had "Fish for Supper!"

Questions for Discussions:
1. What did the mother do at the beach?
2. Name two songs they sang.
3. How did God show his love?
4. How big was the fish?
5. Did they share the blessing?
6. Tell of a blessing you have shared.

A Fearful Night

*The angel of the LORD encampeth round about them
that fear him, and delivereth them. Psalms 34:7*

May 5, 1962. *El Cinco de Mayo* is a day of extraordinary celebration in Mexico. It commemorates the Mexican army's victory over the French forces of Napoleon III, on May 5, 1862, at the Battle of Puebla. The festivities include parades with elaborate floats, street dancing in brightly colored costumes of the era, feasting, revelry, and fireworks.

We had recently moved to Rosarito Beach and knew nothing of what was going on in the town three miles away. Our day had been normal. I took care of the children and James visited those who seemed interested in knowing more about God. His visiting included daily Bible reading with Tomas and his brother Pedro.

Rosi had been sick for many weeks, but now she was feeling better. While Bobby and Rudy watched her, Tricia, Mary, Shirley and I went out into the fields and gathered wild flowers. In the afternoon the neighbor children came over and together with Bobby, Timmy, and Tricia, they created their own parade. They marched back and forth on the driveway behind our houses. Some boys had sticks—make believe guns—over their shoulders, some were beating on tin cans or their mother's cooking pots as if they were drums. Bobby wore a cute hat and carried his toy rifle while Timmy, toddling beside him, had on one of James' hats that all but covered his eyes. One of the larger boys carried Tricia on his shoulders calling out as they paraded, *"La reina. La reina,"* (the queen). I suppose they were celebrating the Cinco de Mayo (although I had no thought of it at that time).

That evening we sang, read the Bible and prayed together in family worship as usual; then we settled down for the night. Sometime during the night, we were awakened by a woman's blood-curdling screams. "It sounds like Cipriana," I whispered.

"Jaime, Jaime! Jaime!" She was screaming.

"Hurry, James," I said, "I think it's my friend needing you."

James and I quickly slipped on our clothes and shoes. Since there was no electricity, everything was pitch dark. James jumped into our car and turned it around so the car headlights shone directly on the door of Cipriana's house. She was standing in the doorway holding her young son. Blood streaked her white skirt, and her hands and arms were spotted with blood. She chattered excitedly while pointing inside the house. James started toward their house. "Do be careful," I cautioned. "Someone inside must have a knife. If you defend her you might get stabbed." Neighbor men came running. Everyone was talking and shouting. However, I could not understand what anyone was saying.

I watched as James and the neighbor entered the house. Soon they came back one on either side of her husband, Salvador. His arms were over their shoulders as he could hardly walk because he was so drunk. Blood from his arm was dripping down on James. Salvador's pants and shirt were splattered with blood. They helped him down the three steps and into the back seat of our car. Cipriana, with her baby, jumped in beside him. "I'll be back," James shouted as they sped out onto the highway and headed toward the hospital in Tijuana.

By now, Mary, Rudy and Shirley were awake and standing behind me looking out the doorway. As soon as James left I closed and locked the door. "Let's pray," I whispered. "Be quiet so we don't wake the little children."

We tiptoed into the side room and got on our knees on the mattress where James and I had been sleeping moments before. I was so thankful to have the teenagers with me on a night like this. We prayed one after another for our protection and for James' safety while driving on the narrow, curvy road. We supposed they were getting close to the hospital in Tijuana about fifteen miles away.

More and more neighbors were gathering outside between our house and Cipriana's. There they talked and talked, while we were praying inside. Their voices sounded angry. Then, little by little, the women's voices died away. I assumed they went back to their homes and sleeping children. The men stayed and the longer they talked, the more afraid I got. I was afraid they were angry with James for taking the man away. I feared they might take revenge on us, his family.

"Lets find some verses about God's protection," I suggested. Bobby was awake now and went to get my Bible while others found their Bibles. "The Lord is my shepherd," Bobby suggested. "I will fear no evil."

"Good," I said.

Rudy found it first and read, "The Lord is my shepherd . . . I will fear no evil: for thou art with me . . . Thou preparest a table before me in the presence of mine enemies."

"Here is another one about fear," Mary said. "I will read it. It's in I John 4:18. 'There is no fear in love; but perfect love casteth out fear: because fear hath torment. He that feareth is not made perfect in love.'"

Shirley was trembling so badly she could hardly speak. "But, but, but, how can we not be afraid in times like this?" she questioned.

"I don't know," I answered, "because I sure am afraid. Let's pray again."

We all prayed again. Then I said, "I think I have read another verse in Psalms about not being afraid."

"Maybe this is it," Rudy said and began reading. "The Lord is my light and my salvation; whom shall I fear? The LORD is the strength of my life; of whom shall I be afraid? When the wicked, even mine enemies and my foes, came upon me to eat up my flesh, they stumbled and fell. Though an host should encamp against me, my heart shall not fear: . . . For in the time of trouble he shall hide me in his pavilion: in the secret of his tabernacle shall he hide me; He shall set me up upon a rock. . . . Therefore will I offer in his tabernacle sacrifices of joy; I will sing, yea, I will sing praises unto the LORD."

"Maybe singing will keep us from being afraid," Mary said. "Shall we sing?"

"But we might wake up the babies," Shirley cautioned.

"I think it is about morning anyway," I said as I pointed toward the only window in the room. "Look, the sky is getting light over the hill."

We sang and our fears faded away.

By noon James had returned and told us that Salvador and his brother were drunk and had gotten into an argument. Salvador wanted to hit his brother, but knew he should not, so he swung his fist away from his brother. Not realizing how close he was to the window, he accidentally hit the window. It broke and ripped his arm open. "The ligaments in his arm were cut in several places. He may never be able to use some of his fingers again," James said sadly. "See what drinking and anger can do! He will regret this day the rest of his life!"

Questions for Discussion:
1. What did the family do on a normal day?
2. What did the children do in the afternoon?
3. What awakened the family?
4. Why did they pray, read the Bible and sing?
5. What brought them the most comfort?
6. What lessons should we learn from this story?

Lost in the Desert—
Trouble Ahead

Trust in the Lord with all thine heart; and lean not unto
thine own understanding. In all thy ways acknowledge
him, and he shall direct thy paths. Proverbs 3:5, 6

It was July, 1962. I cooked the last bit of corn meal mush,
and we ate it without milk. James and I went outside to start
the usual day's laundry. "I know God will send us money for
groceries today," James said, as he was filling the wash tubs
with water from the water barrel sitting beside the door.

"If he doesn't," I added rather negatively, "we'll eat boiled
potatoes and split pinto beans for lunch and after that we
will have only split beans. The children are really tired of our
menus."

"It won't ever be that bad," he said reproving me for my
lack of faith.

As I re-entered the house for more dirty clothes, I heard
a car stop on the dirt driveway behind our little three-room
house. I looked up and saw Brother Harland Smith.

"Hello, James," he called through the open window of his
white '59 Chevy pickup.

James, so thrilled to see the jubilant face of his friend,
hurried toward him. They had been acquainted for several

years, but only recently had James learned the uniqueness of this energetic man who was already out of his pickup and shaking James' hand.

"How is my brother?" he asked.

"Just fine," James answered. "We are keeping busy and happy to serve the Lord."

"Is every thing okay?"

I wondered how James would answer that one. We had promised each other that we would tell only God about our needs. As soon as James got his wits together he answered, "The family is well and we are thankful for God's blessings."

"No one had the flu?" Brother Smith asked as he fumbled through the glove compartment of the pickup. He brought out several letters and handed them to James.

"No one has had the flu," James replied.

"I've been awfully sick, that is why I haven't been down for several weeks. Now I'm snowed under with work, but I just had to take off today to come and see you. I hoped if everything is all right so that you could be away a few days, maybe you would like to take a load of things out to the Indian reservation. This is the most difficult time of year for them. I know some may be almost starving by now. I brought along 400 pounds of potatoes and 200 pounds of split dry beans. These should help them through until their gardens start producing again. There are several boxes of clothing also to give out wherever they are needed."

"I'll be glad to do that," James said as they were walking inside.

We sat down at the table, and Bro. Harland began his usual inspirational talks. He could speak about any subject and turn the hearts of his audience toward God. The next hour seemed like minutes to us. He encouraged us and renewed our faith, our love, and our hope in our mighty and loving God.

"Well, I must be going; although, I'd love to stay longer. I have much work to do, and it is a four hour drive back home to Pomona. Maybe I'll get a little done before dark."

He tore a check out of his check book and said, "If you have enough gas to drive to Ensenada, you can cash this at the gas station where I usually do business. This should cover the expenses of the trip."

We bowed in prayer, and the angels seemed to join us. He prayed, "Make yourself real to this family as you were real to the people of Bible times when you rained food from heaven, made iron to float, caused a donkey to talk, shut the hungry lions' mouths, and caused the flour bin to always have flour. God, you said, 'The cattle on a thousand hills are yours.' Now please, God, supply their every need, whatever it may be. Amen!"

Then saying, "Good-bye and God bless you," to each of us individually, he jumped into his white truck and drove away. We watched until he was out of sight.

When we opened the letters, there was a check for groceries as James had said would come that day.

"How did he know we needed food?" Mary Ellen asked, as we were scrubbing the clothes.

"He didn't know. God knew, and God impressed someone to send money in their letter."

"Who would like to go along with me to the Indian Reservation?" James asked, after he had checked over the 1952 Chevy panel truck. "The truck runs good and we should make the trip fine."

Everyone wanted to go except me. It seemed foolish to expose the children to the extreme heat of the desert in July. Also, one or two of them usually got carsick when zigzagging back and forth around the mountains. But, neither did I want to stay home alone with the two babies, Tim and Rosi. I knew Bob and Tricia really wanted to go with him.

The road to the reservation would take us over high, dangerous mountains and a hot, dusty desert. Many miles of our road were part of the Baja 500 and Baja 1000 off road race trails. The dusty roads choked me up until I could hardly breathe. On the other hand, any change from the depressing routine we had been through the last few weeks would be great. *Oh, Lord I prayed, What should I do? Is it too selfish of me to ask James to spend another day getting groceries for me while others are awaiting a meager ration to keep from starving? (James would have to go to Ensenada, the only place he could cash the check we received in the mail. That would take the remainder of this day.) Yes, I knew that would be too selfish. To stay home or to go would be a hardship, but I am willing to do either, Lord, if you will be with me."*

While the older children were getting their things packed, I grabbed the Bible and went to my place of prayer. I let the Bible fall open and my eyes fell on a verse in Acts that said something about going, ". . .but trouble and affliction await thee." There was my message! His will was for me to go, but expect trouble. *Okay, Lord, I will go because I know there is no trouble that you can't help us through.*

I retraced my steps to the house and quickly gathered up clean diapers, evaporated milk, baby bottles and a change of clothing for each of us, for we would be coming back tomorrow, or the following day. There was no need for camping equipment as we would stay in the mission station.

"There has been no rain for several weeks, so the dirt roads should be in excellent condition," James said as we turned on to the main highway. "It's four o'clock, so we should be there by nine, before dark. We'll get food and fill our water jug in Ensenada after we get gasoline and cash the check Bro. Smith gave us for expenses."

Questions for Discussion:
  1. What was the family's problem?
  2. Who did God send to help them?
  3. What did the Indians need?
  4. What was James asked to do?
  5. Did money come as James had said?
  (to be continued)

THE BROKEN WATER JUG

All the paths of the LORD are mercy and truth unto such
as keep his covenant and his testimonies. Psalms 25:10

Because we had no money to pay for the toll road, we followed
the narrow highway that wound its way along the rugged Baja
coast line. In some places we were near sea level. At other
places, we looked over almost vertical cliffs to the sea shore
some 250 feet below. At those heights, I wondered what kind
of trouble was awaiting us. Turning inland, we zigzagged
our way up a steep mountain to a high plateau of 1,000 feet
elevation. We crossed the plateau, and then we wound down
the mountain on Tiger Tail Road before entering the port
city of Ensenada. It was located on a beautiful bay with tall
rugged mountains surrounding it.

In Ensenada, we often stopped to see the ocean freighters
that come in and out from different parts of the world. Today
we hurried on to the gas station to fill the truck with gasoline
and cash our two checks. Brother Harland Smith had given
us one for expenses and another had come in the mail. The
elderly Russian woman, who owned and managed the gas
station, greeted us warmly. "What a nice big family!" She said
as she hugged each of us.

By 6:00 p.m. we had passed Ensenada's city dump east of the city where the blacktop road ended. We were leaving behind the fresh cool ocean breeze and heading to the desert in hot July weather. We were now getting on the Baja 500 off road race trails. In some places the road was only wide enough for one vehicle. When we crested peaks or rounded blind curves, we prayed and honked, saying, "I'm coming, clear the road!" As we bumped along the rutted road, I thought how blessed the Indian are in the United States. No matter where they live, our government provides them food and other things that they need.

The dark brown, uninsulated panel truck seemed to be like a magnet, drawing every ray of the July sun inside, thus making it feel like an oven. Each person was bathed in his own perspiration. The van had no windows to open in the back. The five gallon water jug was in constant use. We drank, and we draped wet wash cloths over our heads and across the back of our necks. We screened out a little of the hot wind by hanging wet towels in the only two windows which were in the cab.

Leaving *Piedras Gordas* (a ranch called Fat Rock) behind, we were winding our way through the mountains, past *Los Minitos,* (an abandoned gold mine), and on down into the valley of *Ojos Negros.* It was a large, irrigated, agriculture valley named Black Eyes. Staying on the main road, which was only a dirt trail, we headed on eastward toward the Santa Catarina Indian Reservation.

"I believe this road is the worst I've seen," James said. "Hang on everybody. There are lots of bumps ahead." Just then, he swerved to miss a big gaping hole in the road.

"Hold the water jug," I yelled.

Rudy grabbed for the jug, but missed it. It fell hard against the metal floor and broke. Our precious water poured under boxes of clothes, sacks of beans and potatoes, suitcases, and bare feet. Now, where in the Baja desert will we be able to find safe drinking water?

After picking up the broken glass from the floor of the truck, James hung the neck of the broken jug on a fence post. "There," he said, "we will leave a reminder on this desert."

"Do you think someone will see it and come bringing us water?" I asked.

"I hope so," Rudy answered. "We'll be thirsty in ten minutes."

"I wonder how long it will hang there?" Mary asked.

"Well, what shall we do? Go back and see if we can find water in Ojos Negros?" James asked. "We have no jug, but maybe we could buy one."

I turned to Shirley. "Are we nearer to the reservation or Ojos Negros?" I asked.

"Maybe closer to the reservation," she answered.

"Then I think we'd better go on," I advised.

Everyone was quiet. I don't know what the others were thinking, but I was trying to think of a place where we could find drinking water. I was also hoping that Tim and Rosi would go to sleep so they wouldn't be thirsty and crying for a drink. Bobby, six, and Tricia, four, were pretty mature for their ages. I thought they would understand and keep quiet. We all knew that there was good water at the mission house on the reservation.

After driving for about another thirty minutes, Shirley questioned rather shyly, "*Sierra Colorado* (Colored Mountain) is to our left, shouldn't it be to the right?"

In the twilight, we could see the mountain. "I must have missed a turn so we're on the road to El Alamo," James said. "We could spend the night there and go on in the morning."

"Yes, please," I pleaded. "We are all parched, tired and hungry."

"This doesn't look like the road to El Alamo either," Shirley said. She had been to El Alamo several times.

"I can tell by the sound of the motor that we are going up a hill. Is there a hill before getting to El Alamo?" James asked.

"No," Shirley answered.

Rosi whimpered. I kissed her forehead. She felt cool. I was thankful the sun had gone down behind the mountains on the other side of *Ojos Negros* and the desert was beginning to cool off.

"We are going into a canyon!" James exclaimed. Sierra Colorado was on our left, and as we were descending, the other mountain was forming a wall on our right.

"Look, a wooden gate across the road!" Bobby shouted.

"Good, there must be a house nearby," I said hopefully.

"Let's stop and pray and let the motor rest a while," James said. "I don't know where to go from here."

We prayed, then let the children run around and play while we discussed which direction we should go.

When we loaded back up and were ready to go, the truck refused to start.

Questions for Discussion:
1. Were they going on a vacation?
2. What were they taking to the Indians?
3. What valuable thing did they lose?
4. How important is water on the desert?
5. What would you do if you were in their situation?

Sleeping on the Sand

I will both lay me down in peace, and sleep: for thou,
LORD, only makest me dwell in safety. Psalms 4:8

We were lost on the Baja California desert somewhere between
Ensenada on the west coast and San Felipe on the east, and
our '52 Chevy panel truck would not start. We were delivering
potatoes and dry beans to the starving Indians.

Thankfully, the July sun had gone down and the air was
beginning to cool off. Nevertheless, with four young children,
ages six and under, three teenagers and no water nor food, it
was frightening.

We decided to push the truck down the canyon trail in
hopes that would cause it to jump start. However, to our
dismay the wooden gate blocking the road opened toward
us and we had rolled almost against it. All of us got out and
together we pushed the truck back up the hill enough so the
gate would open. Then we rolled the truck all the way to the
bottom of the hill, but the motor refused to start.

"I guess we are spending the night here," James said.

"But we have no water," I protested. Two-year-old Timmy
leaned his head against my leg and cried, "Drink, Mommy,
drink." I patted his cheek that was wet with sweat. I handed
Rosi to Mary Ellen and picked him up. To divert his attention

from his thirst I pointed to the stars and the big moon and said, "Look at the bright moon that God made." As the words left my mouth, I felt calmness in my trembling spirit. I knew the God who created the moon would help us; He will quench Tim's thirst. Tim never asked again for a drink until we had water.

"Let's pray again," James said.

We were desperate to get God's attention, so we all knelt in the sand. As I listened to others praying, my mind wandered back to my childhood. I recalled the stories my mother had read to me about God supplying food and water for the children of Israel when they were crossing a desert. She always assured me that if I lived to please God, He would do for me as He did for the people in Bible times. I searched myself to see that I had been pleasing Him in my actions and attitudes. I saw that I had many hidden faults. *Oh, God, forgive me for the times I have disappointed you in my thinking, actions, or my attitude; and please, take care of us like you did the people of Israel,* I begged silently.

Above the soft voices of the children praying, I could hear coyotes howling. Before we were up off our knees, James said, "Better gather some sticks and start a fire. There are lions and bobcats around here, too. They told me that one of the Indian boys killed a big bobcat the other day. A fire will give us some protection from hungry animals."

"Do you think we'll be here long enough for potatoes to bake in the coals of fire?" I asked.

"We'll be here all night, dear. The truck battery is dead," he replied.

"I don't want to stay all night with the wild dogs," Tricia pleaded. She was clinging to me.

"They won't hurt us," I said. "They are afraid of fire."

In the darkness, the mountain on the South appeared to be a vertical wall, but the one to the North rose gradually.

After James built a fire, he picked up the flashlight and started climbing up the mountain. "Let's see if we can see a light from a house close by," he said. Rudy, Bobby, Shirley, and Mary followed him. I could see him carefully scanning the bushes ahead of them continually for any sign of wild animals.

I sat down by the campfire, with baby Rosi in my arms, Tim and Tricia huddling on either side, and I sang:

> *I'll not be afraid for the terror by night,*
> *Nor the arrow that flieth by day;*
> *For the Lord Whom I serve is my shield and my*
> *light,*
> *He will guide and protect all the way.*
> *I'll not be afraid, I'll not be afraid*
> *Where he leadeth I safely can go;*
> *I will trust him alway both by night and by day*
> *He'll be with me forever I know.*

Inside I was shaking, however, for the children's sake, I dared not act afraid.

A cool wind began blowing. *Just like the desert,* I thought. It is very hot in the day and cold at night. I went to the truck to get some old clothes to wrap around us. As I looked back toward the campfire, I saw Tricia and Timmy singing together.

> *Me not be 'fraid.*
> *Me not be 'fraid,*
> *De Lord me serve is me*
> *wheel and me 'ight.*

As they sang, my fear left, for I knew God would not desert such trusting children.

As the others came back down the mountain, I heard them singing:

If it wasn't for the Lord,
Tell me what would I do?
Tell me what would I do?
He is everything to me,
He is bread in dry places.
He is water in a thirsty land.
He is my rock and shelter
And He holds me by the hand.

We all sat down around the fire and sang it again. After that no one complained of being thirsty or afraid.

With unwashed hands, we peeled away the ash covered potato peelings and sucked out the soft potato. Each of us ate the dry potato, but no one asked for a drink!!!

It was getting cold and the only warm clothing in the boxes was some men's suit jackets. Everyone put one on! Bobby's reached to his shoe tops, but Tricia and Tim's made trails in the sand wherever they walked. We put more wood on the fire and told stories. One by one the children fell asleep; then we put them inside the panel truck for the remainder of the night. The rest of us kept singing and talking around the fire until we, too, began nodding. "We'll need to keep this fire going all night to keep the wild animals away," James said. "Whenever anyone wakes up, be sure to put more wood on it." Then using clothes from the boxes for sleeping bags and pillows, we laid over in the sand and attempted to get some sleep. Throughout the night, I could hear the coyotes howling.

As the first bit of light came over the Sierra Colorado Mountain, I awoke and put more unwashed potatoes in the ashes around the camp fire. As soon as it was light enough to read, we read the Bible and prayed together. Then James began trying to get the truck started. Shirley, Mary Ellen, Rudy and Bobby climbed the mountain again in search of a house.

"There's smoke rising from a clump of trees!" they shouted.

"Oh! Wonderful!" James exclaimed, and raced up the mountain to see. "Look it's curling up like smoke from a chimney! And see that red spot? It might be the roof of a house," he said.

Shirley could speak a little Spanish, so we chose her to go investigate. "Take this compass and be sure to follow its direction," James explained. "According to it, that house is east. When you come back, come directly west and you won't get lost, even if the compass is not exactly right."

Mary Ellen went with Shirley. I checked the time. It was 6:30 a.m. They should be back by 8:00 or 9:00 a.m. As I watched them disappear, I prayed, *Please Lord, protect them and keep them from getting lost.*

Questions for Discussion:
1. Where was the family?
2. Why did they build a fire?
3. What song did the little children sing?
4. How did the children's singing affect the mother?
5. What did they do around the camp fire?
6. Did God protect them while they slept?

Food and Water

But my God shall supply all your need according to
his riches in glory by Christ Jesus. Philippians 4:19

Shirley and Mary Ellen had been gone hunting for help for
about three hours. I started checking the road for them.
By 10:00 a.m. they still had not returned, so I climbed the
mountain hoping to spot them. I saw nothing of the girls
and was almost back down when James called. "Come here,
I need your help."

James had been working on the truck since early morning.
He had checked the gas. The tank was half-full. He had
cleaned the points and each spark plug. While he was doing
this, I carried Rosi back and forth between him and the other
children, who were playing contentedly in the sand under a
tree.

Although it had been fourteen hours since having anything
to drink, no one had asked for water. Neither had baby Rosi
cried for a bottle of milk.

"We're going to pretend this truck is a lawn mower," James
said. "I've jacked up the rear wheel and taken off the tire.
Now we will pull this rope that I have coiled around the
wheel. Rudy, you sit in the cab and push the choke in when
the motor starts."

James took the end of the rope and said, "Line up in front of me and grab the rope. When I say, 'pull,' we will pull at the same time. Okay, let's go. One, two, three, PULL!" We pulled; the rope slipped and James sat down hard, I fell on his lap and Bobby on me, all of us in a stack!

While he was wrapping the rope to try again, I took another look down the road for the girls. Nothing! We pulled on the rope and fell on top of one another again, then again, and again. But the motor only coughed!

Finally at 11:15, the girls came back with a little short dark Mexican and a team of beady-eyed horses, "¿*Caballos le ayudo?*" (Horses help you?) he asked.

James looked at the pair of nervous, wild-eyed horses and knew it wouldn't do to hook them just six feet behind the tail pipe of our noisy panel truck. "Caballos no, gracias," (horses no thank you) James answered. "*Hombre sí*" (Man yes). He pointed to the man and then to the rope in his hand.

The man tied his horses to a tree and returned to help us. "Now if everyone will help pull, I think this rig will start." This time there were six in the line, and James working the choke. Everyone pulled backwards at the same time as hard as possible. We kept wrapping the rope and pulling, wrapping the rope and pulling. I think on about the twentieth try, the motor finally started! "Thank the Lord!" we all shouted.

Shirley then asked the man where we could find water. He led us on down the road to a fresh water spring where watercress was growing around the edges of a pool. "Please God, make this water pure for us," James prayed as he filled cup after cup and handed it to the thirsty children.

I filled a clean bottle for Rosi and added her formula. "I'm trusting that this won't make you sick," I said and kissed her damp forehead.

After washing our hands, faces, necks and ears, we sat in the shade and munched sprigs of watercress. The man, looking puzzled, said, "You people are different. You are lost and having car problems in a strange country, and you are not afraid."

"It is because we are children of God," Shirley helped James explain. "God is our father. He has kept us from being hungry or thirsty. It's been seventeen hours since these children have had a drink. Would you like to serve a God like that? I have a book that will help you get acquainted with Him." James took a New Testament from the truck and gave it to the man.

"Gracias," the man exclaimed, and then said something to Shirley. Shirley told us that he had said, "I've been wanting one of these books for a long time."

It was early afternoon now and we loaded up in the oven-hot panel truck, but nobody complained. We were happy to at last be on the trail again finding our way to the Santa Catarina Indian Reservation to which we had hoped to arrive at yesterday.

Following the man's instructions, we went back the way we had come until we came to a fork in the road. There we followed the road to the right.

Soon we came upon a ranch house. We stopped to confirm the directions given to us by the man. A short, plump woman met us at the door and invited us to come in and sit down. The only place to sit was around a table with benches much like a picnic table. Hurrying back to her oven, she took out a pan of hot sweet biscuits. These she placed before us and motioned for us to eat. They tasted somewhat like sugar cookies. Then she placed nine tall glasses on the table and filled each one with cold milk from a bucket sitting at the far end of the table. We had been warned to never drink unpasteurized milk in Mexico, but we could not refuse the children such a treat when they were so hungry. We bowed our heads and thanked God for bringing us to this generous woman and we asked Him to bless her and sanctify the milk.

In broken Spanish we explained to the woman that our panel truck had broken down, that we had been lost, and that we slept all night on the sand around our camp fire. She raised her eyebrows and looked afraid. Then Shirley told her we had broken our water jug the day before and how God had kept the children from being thirsty for seventeen hours. The woman smiled almost in disbelief, but then she brought us a gallon jug of cool water from her gas powered refrigerator. "This is good spring water for you," she said and put it in Shirley's hand. We tried to pay her but she shook her head, no, and began talking excitedly in Spanish. Shirley understood her to say that she was very happy to have visitors. "Often a week passes without me seeing another person."

"Muchas gracias," (Many thanks) we told her. Then James wrote our names in a New Testament and gave it to her. She smiled happily and said, *"Muchas, muchas gracias,"* (Many, many thanks).

Questions for Discussion:
1. How many hours were they without water?
2. What had the man, who helped them, been wanting?
3. Do you see God's mercy for this man?
4. Why was the woman happy?
5. Name some good that came from this trouble.
   (to be continued)

HOME AGAIN

Men ought always to pray, and not to faint; Luke 18:1b

We were again on the hot desert road, which was only two shallow ruts in the loose sand. In a short while, we met a truck. James, trying to share the road, drove out of the ruts to let the truck pass. Immediately, we found ourselves STUCK IN THE SAND. We were hidden by the dust which the truck left behind. We could hear the sound of its motor as it faded away in the distance. We had no hopes of seeing another vehicle. The woman at the house we just left had said, "Often a week passes without me seeing another person." We would all be dead in a week. God would have to create another miracle if He wanted to use us longer.

I knew the children would be overcome by the heat if I didn't get them out of the truck, but there were no trees for shade anywhere in sight. I wondered if it might be hotter standing in the desert sun than in the van. To make some shade, I took the suit jackets we had used for covers the night before and spread them over a nearby mesquite bush. Then I spread layers of jackets on the sand to keep it from burning their feet. I stood them under this scant shade.

We all worked desperately shoveling sand from under the truck and from around the tires hoping to get the truck out.

The sand burned our feet through our shoes and our wash-cloth hats kept falling off. "We have done everything we can except pray," James said. Of course, we were praying in our hearts.

'Oh, God," he begged desperately, "I don't need to tell you how badly we need Your help. We can't stay here very long, or we will all die. We're hot and helpless...." Before he finished praying we heard a rumbling sound.

Across the desert toward the South we saw a cloud of dust. We were watching the cloud get nearer as Rudy was climbing up on top of the truck. "It's a pickup! And it's coming our way!" he shouted from his lookout point, standing on the roof of the panel truck.

Minutes later, it stopped beside us and the driver shouted, "*¿Qué pasó?*" (What happened?)

James pointed to the truck buried to the axle in the sand. The man quickly hooked a chain to our truck and pulled it backward out into the ruts again. "You're lucky we came along," the driver said in Spanish. Then sped away.

"This wasn't luck," Rudy said, as we were gathering up children and umbrella-coats. "God answered our prayers and sent you along at just the time He knew we would be needing some help."

By the time he had sped away, it was getting toward evening, so we decided to stay the night in El Alamo.

El Alamo was a picturesque village nestled at the foot of the Sierra Madre Mountains. There was an old deserted gold mine on its west side. Of the many homes that dotted the landscape, only a few were occupied.

In the days of the gold rush, El Alamo had five active gold mines around the city and a population of over five thousand, but now scarcely one hundred people lived there. Brother R. J. Elliott, a companion of D.S. Warner, preached in El Alamo in about the year 1900. He entered the town tired and hungry after walking twenty-six miles to bring the gospel to them. However, he was treated very rudely by the American miners and the owner of the mines offered him no food nor lodging. There were also many Chinese men working the mines. A kind Chinese cook gave him a piece of pie, brought him a blanket, and let him sleep on the table that night. The American mineworkers were rough and ungodly. However, when Brother Elliott preached, a hush fell over them, and they listened. Brother Elliott thought the Mexicans seemed hungry for the Gospel because they bought all the Bibles and New Testaments which he had carried in on his pack donkey. At the time, he could not speak much Spanish. He also thought the Indians accepted The Gospel in their hearts, even though he could not converse with them either.

Brother Elliott was disheartened with El Alamo. When leaving the city he prayed, "Lord, let there someday be a Church of God in this place."

Some seventy years later those prayers were answered when a group of saints led by Bro. Harland Smith raised up a congregation there. For several years there were camp meetings held with good attendances. People came from Santa Catarina, El Rodeo, La Huerta, and other settlements around El Alamo. The church building and mission house were built at the east edge of the town close to the entrance to the village.

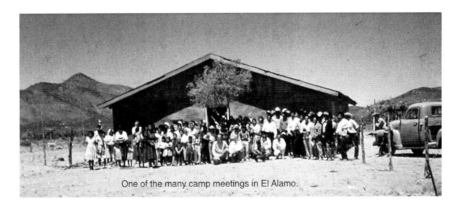

One of the many camp meetings in El Alamo.

Another meeting in El Alamo   Edith Cole

Bobby

Harland Smith

Although few people lived in El Alamo, it had the largest store in all the desert area. Both Indians and Mexicans came to buy their provisions at the store in El Alamo unless they were fortunate enough to get a ride all the way to Ensenada.

El Alamo's store had two small shelves of canned food, unwrapped bread, packaged crackers, and soaps for bath or laundry. There were the usual staple foods such as flour, sugar, salt, oats, rice, beans, and of course, chili peppers. One could also purchase hardware items, such as buckets, wash basins, tubs, ropes, knives, and gasoline kept in a barrel outside.

Darkness was settling over us when we drove up in front of the church near 9:00 p.m. (Since yesterday around 5:00 p.m. we had only eaten ash covered potatoes, one cookie, and a glass of milk. God had taken the hunger and thirst away from the children. Not one of them, ages one through six had begged for food or water.) We made a *poor man's feast* from canned vegetables that we found in the mission house and a few things James bought from the store.

While at the store, James discovered several in the congregation were sick and had been hoping someone would come to minister and pray for them. Now we knew, at least in part, why God allowed us to miss the road and end up in El Alamo.

He went visiting that night. The following morning, after visiting the sick again, we started out for the Indian Reservation at Santa Catarina. We arrived there without any more trouble.

What might be called the center of the reservation was the one-room school house where Sister Edith Cole taught the children. There was also a three-room mission house and three other family dwellings near the creek dam which Brother Harland Smith, Brother Barney Whittenborn and others had constructed.

Immediately, James and Rudy began visiting the people and delivering the beans and potatoes. Houses made from either adobe blocks, or sticks plastered with mud, were scattered among miles of rolling desert hills. Because their homes were so far apart, it took all of the remaining day and most of the next day to distribute food to each family.

On Thursday we said good-bye to the Indians and started back to our home in Rosarito Beach. The trip home took a little over five hours, including shopping for food in Ensenada.

As we were getting unpacked, one of our neighbors brought us our mail. There were letters from each of our parents, Alvin and Mabel Hightower, H.P and Agnes Huskey. Another letter came from a friend and one from a stranger. The one from the stranger had a check for enough money to buy our family a generous month's supply of groceries!

Questions for Discussion:
1. Why did they get stuck in the sand?
2. Is it always best to be courteous to others?
3. Is spreading the Gospel always profitable?
4. How far did George Elliott walk to bring Bibles to El Alamo?
5. Did God answer George Elliott's prayers?
6. Tell of some prayers God has answered for you.

Spreading God's Word

I am not ashamed of the gospel of Christ:
for it is the power of God unto salvation to
everyone that believeth; . . . Romans 1:16

"Say, Josefina, what's happened to Esteven?" Ramon asked. "He hasn't been over to play cards in three days."

"It's that book. Just look at him," she said as she pointed toward the other room where Esteven was sitting by the window with a book in his hands. Esteven never looked up.

"He pays no attention to anyone; he just reads from morning until night. Every minute that he isn't working he's reading. I can hardly get him to eat."

Ramon put his head through the opening and whistled. Esteven looked up and smiled, then continued reading. "How could any book be more interesting than a good game of Poker?" Ramon asked.

"This book gives me the answers to questions I've had since I was a child," Esteven answered. "You remember when we had to memorize the catechism before taking our First Communion? The Sisters told us to listen and not ask questions. In this book, I'm finding answers to some of my questions about Jesus. It tells me who Jesus Christ is, why

He died, and that Jesus himself was baptized after he was a grown man."

"Esteven, are you taking up a false religion? Did you get that book from the American?"

"Sure did."

"But, you know we Mexicans are all Catholic. Our fathers, our grandfathers, and our great grandfathers were Catholic. Why do you want to change?" Ramon asked.

"I never understood our father's religion. We say prayers, and we confess to men who are meaner than I am. We light candles. We eat fish on Friday. But I never knew why. I think I can understand that American guy's religion better than ours."

"I think you are getting yourself into a ton of trouble that you will later have to confess to the priest," Ramon said, cautioning Esteven.

"I'm not so sure we need to confess to a priest. Just read this." Esteven handed Ramon the New Testament. It was opened to 1 John chapter one.

Ramon read aloud, "*The blood of Jesus Christ his Son cleanseth us from all sin. If we say we have no sin, we deceive ourselves, and the truth is not in us. If we confess our sins, he is faithful and just to forgive us our sins, and to cleanse us from all unrighteousness. If we say that we have not sinned we make him a liar and his word is not in us. My little children, these things I write into you, that ye sin not. And if any man sin, we have an advocate with the Father, Jesus Christ the righteous: And he is the propitiation for our sins: and not for ours only, but also for the sins of the whole world.*' Wow! That is awesome!" Ramon explained.

"You see, Jesus isn't angry with us as we have been taught. He is our helper, and He is our Savior."

"You really believe so?" Ramon asked.

"Yes, something inside of me says it is true," Esteven said.

"I think I'd like to read your book. Can I borrow it?"

"No, no, I can't part with it. Maybe you could also get one. Go to their meetings and just ask them for one," Esteven told Ramon.

Ramon came with Esteven the following Sunday and asked for a Bible. I don't remember if we had an extra Bible for him at that time, but I do know we gave him one as soon as we had one. Later, his wife told me that he had stayed up all night reading it.

Ramon and Esteven are just two examples of the many people who received free Bibles the first year that we lived in Rosarito. When we moved there a huge hydroelectric plant was being constructed. Hundreds of men from different states all over Mexico were coming there seeking jobs. A great many of these men received employment. Many worked for a short time while others worked for long periods of time. Most all of these men returned to their homes in different parts of Mexico. Some returned to stay and others returned only to visit their families.

While these men were in Rosarito, many came and heard the Gospel for the first time. Our tiny house would be full and others would be standing outside. James stood in the doorway so both those inside and those listening outside could hear the Word of God. His Spanish was so limited that most of his sermons consisted of reading passages from the different books of the Bible. Many of these men had respect and reverence for God and they desired to have a Bible of their own. Some said it was their most prized possession. Others asked for more information about this 'new religion' as they called it. James would explain as best he could about the plan of salvation and repentance. Sometimes he would pray with them. They were given a New Testament or a Bible if they wanted one.

It is marvelous that God supplied so many Bibles to be given away. It was also amazing that God sent us to live in the spot where so many men came to services for a few weeks or months and then went back to their homes in other states carrying a Bible to an area where salvation by faith had not been heard. In this way the Word of God was scattered throughout a country where in years past reading a Bible had been banned.

I thank God that He showed James that we should move to Rosarito Beach even though we knew nothing about the people, the electric plant, nor the many men who were coming and going from the city. Seeking God's will and obeying God is always the best.

Questions for Discussion:
1. Why had Esteven not been visiting his friend?
2. What had Esteven learned by reading the Bible?
3. Why were many men coming to Rosarito?
4. What did the men do who did not get a job?
5. How did God's Word get scattered over Mexico?
6. Is it important that each family have a Bible?

STRANDED IN THE DESERT

Be strong and of a good courage, fear not, nor
be afraid of them: for the LORD thy God,
he it is that doth go with thee; he will not fail
thee, nor forsake thee. Deuteronomy 31:6

On an August afternoon, 1962, we were again delivering food
to the starving Pai-pai Indians in Baja California. Because it
was nearing harvest time, the Indians' food supply was very
scant.

On our last trip in July, we had gotten lost before finding
the reservation. This trip we were happy that we had stayed
on the right road, and according to our odometer we were
nearing our destination when our 1952 Chevy panel truck
jerked, coughed, and died. The large port city of Ensenada
(on the Pacific Ocean) was about sixty miles behind us to
the west and San Felipe, a fishing resort (on the Gulf of
California), was about sixty or seventy miles to the east of
where we broke down. Those were the nearest places that we
knew of to find help for an ailing vehicle. To make matters
even worse, we had with us our four small children (ages one
through six).

"Looks like we'll be here until the sun goes down and the coolness of the evening causes the gasoline to flow again," James said. "The panel truck is vapor locked."

"What is that?" I questioned.

"Vapor lock is when the fuel pump and fuel lines get so hot that the liquid gasoline changes to vapor gas and stops the flow of the gasoline. The engine will not run because the gasoline spray cannot be controlled properly," James explained.

I panicked! "In this heat? Our children could become dehydrated within hours. I'm sure it must be 120º! There is no shade. These scrubby mesquite trees and even the taller ones cast only lines of shadows, no real shade."

"It is best not to stay in this windowless van where the heat is more intense," James said, "Let's get everyone out."

Bobby and Tricia climbed out. I pulled Rosi (asleep on her blanket) close to the two open side doors and climbed out with Tim in my arms.

"The sand is burning my feet through my shoes," I complained.

"Mine are burning, too," Bobby added.

"I know," James answered, "but I can't do anything about it. Our ice is already melted, and the water is hot. The gasoline has to cool before the motor will start."

"If God doesn't work a miracle we'll all die," I groaned. I wondered what my Dad would say if one of his grandchildren died of dehydration. Would he be able to forgive James and me for bringing them into this danger? I began praying.

The Santa Catarina Reservation is located in a valley at the foot of the Sierra de San Padre Martin Mountains in the north-central part of the Baja California Peninsula. It is about fifty miles south of the mouth of the Colorado River. Brother Barney and Sister Virginia Whittenborn had discovered the reservation after reading about it in a 1958 issue of *Desert* magazine. A few years later, the Saints built a dam on a little creek so some the indians could have irrigation water for their crops. They also built the mission house in which Sister Edith Cole was now living while teaching in the nearby school building.

We had hardly gotten over the initial shock of being stranded and unprotected from the intense desert sun when we heard something. James and I both opened our eyes wide and looked at each other. Neither said a word, but we were both thinking, *Could it possibly be the motor of a car?* We listened. Still speechless. It was getting louder. The sound was more distinct. "It sounds like a Jeep," James said, his voice escalating with excitement.

A few moments later, a jeep rounded a curve and stopped behind us. Two surprised Americans jumped out at the same time. "What on earth are you doing here?" They asked. "We thought we were blazing a trail, and that we were the first US citizens to cross the peninsula at this point."

The van vapor locked 50 miles from help. Using this stranger's cold grapefruit, it started again.

Now this is almost impossible to believe, but using a cold grapefruit from the stranger's ice chest, James got the gas in the carburetor cooled off and the old truck started again. We shouted, "Praise God!"

I believe we were on the road again in less than a half-hour. In another half-hour we were cooling off inside the mission house at Santa Catarina.

Lindy, the woman in the jeep, took our picture and sent it to us.

"Be strong and of a good courage, fear not, nor be afraid of them: for the Lord thy God he it is that doth go with thee; he will not fail thee, nor forsake thee."

Questions for Discussion:
1. Where was the family going?
2. What were they taking?
3. How far was it to a car repair business?
4. How long did they wait for help?
5. Do you think God sent help?
6. What did God promise?

Strange Gifts

Give, and it shall be given unto you; good measure, pressed down, and shaken together, and running over, shall men give into your bosom. For with the same measure that ye mete withal it shall be measured to you again. Luke 6:38

One day, a friend said to James and me, "I have a donkey I think your children would enjoy." We also thought the children would like to have it so we asked our neighbor, Miguel Esquier, to get it for us. Soon he brought the *burro* to us in his pickup. Excitedly, we gathered around the back of the truck to see our new pet. "Is it big enough to pull a cart?" Bobby asked. "He looks so little."

"I'm sure he is. Donkeys are very strong for their size. That's why they are called *pack animals*," James answered.

"Can we buy a cart so he can pull us in it?" Tim asked.

"Maybe later, but first we will need to train the burro to be obedient."

"What shall we name him?" I asked.

"Mike," Tim suggested.

"No," Bobby stormed. "That was our dog's name."

At that moment, Miguel said, "Step back, so many people are exciting him." Miguel stepped up on the running board of his pickup and reached over the side rails to fasten a rope onto the burro's neck. The burro whirled quickly around and kicked the side rail with both hind feet. Miguel leaped off just in time. He then went to the other side of the pickup and this time he tried to tie a longer rope onto him. The *burro* did the same trick again. Miguel, who had handled other frightened animals, thought he knew what to do. He told us to go where the donkey could not see us. We did, and before long, he had the *burro* tied to a stake driven deep into the ground. "That *burro* is very frightened. This may have been the first time he has ridden in a vehicle," Miguel said. "He will soon calm down and then you will be able to pet him. Just keep everyone away from him for a few days."

An hour or so later Bobby took a bucket of water to the *burro*. The *burro* bit at Bobby and kicked over the bucket of water. "You dumb animal!" Bobby snorted. "I'm not bringing you another drink. It is too hard to pull the bucket of water out of the well." When he entered the house, he said, "Mama, you'd better keep Rosi and Tim away from that *burro*; look, he tried to bite me." I looked at the wet spot on Bobby's shirt and I thought, that sort of a pet won't work for us.

After weeks of good care, the *burro* had not changed. He kicked at every one and tried to bite them when they were least expecting it. We heard remarks like:

"That burro is going to kill some little child."

"Why are you keeping such a dangerous animal?"

"He is an old animal that has been abused," someone said.

"He will never change," another man remarked.

It became dangerous to have Sunday school with the *burro* so near the house. It was almost impossible to keep every child away from it. We tried giving him away, but no one seemed to believe they could tame him. Finally we asked Bro. Harland's advice, "I believe the San Diego Zoo will buy old animals," he said.

"And for what?" I asked.

The children wanted a burro like this one.

"I've heard lions love them," he said.

After all attempts to tame the donkey or to donate it to someone in Mexico had failed, we took him to the San Diego Zoo.

Soon after we were rid of the *burro*, someone offered us a milk cow. We thought that was wonderful! Our children needed more fresh milk! There was a large open field north of the mission house. We could stake it around in different places in that field during the winter and spring. In the summer when the grass dried up we could buy hay. We made a deal, offering to give them a little money for it.

When our milk cow arrived we hurried out to see it just as we had done when the *burro* came. "It is a long horn," Bobby shouted. "Wow!"

"Not a real long horn," James corrected. "Just a cow with long horns."

"She looks mean," Tricia said, and hid behind me.

I gazed at the light brown bony cow. Not at all what I had imagined we might be getting. Her beady eyes flashed back and forth as if trying to decide which of her enemies she would attack first. I took Tim by one hand and Rosi by the other and headed for the house. Tricia followed closely. I wanted them safe in the house when the cow was let out of the truck. Once safe inside, we cracked the door open a little to see out. (The window openings in the mission house were covered with black tar-paper.)

Through the crack of the door we watched the cowboy tie the long rope that was around the cow's neck to the pickup. Then he opened the tailgate. The cow bellowed and looked fearfully at the ramp, then backed away. The two cowboys jumped into the truck and tried pushing her down the ramp. She tried goring them, so they jumped out of the truck onto the ground. Next they both pulled her down the ramp with the rope. She bellowed all the way. However, when her feet hit the solid ground, she zoomed away like lightning. The rope tied to the truck snapped as if it were a piece of string.

One cowboy leaped into the truck cab. The other jumped up into the truck bed, and he began swinging his rope over his head as the truck sped away after the cow. They bounced over sand dunes and around scrub mesquite bushes trying to rope the cow. Sometimes the rope landed on her back and once it fell over her horns, but she managed to get loose. Away they chased it across the field to the fence. The cow jumped the fence and ran across the divided highway without being hit by a car. She disappeared still running toward the mountains. The boys sped back by our house and shouted, "We're going to the mountains to get her."

That was the last time we saw our new milk cow.

We were both disappointed and relieved at the same time.

Questions for Discussion:
1. Are gifts always what we think they will be?
2. Should we be grateful even if we do not like the gift?
3. Should we try to understand the gift giver?
4. Does God command that we give?
5. What will we receive if we give grudgingly?
6. What will the person receive who gives freely?
7. How do you give?

Arrested!

*And when they bring you unto the . . . magistrates . . .
take ye no thought how or what thing ye shall answer,
or what ye shall say: for the Holy Ghost shall teach you
in the same hour what ye ought to say. Luke 12:11, 12*

May 1963. My mind was in a whirl as I watched the police
car speed away from the mission house in Rosarito Beach,
Mexico. They were taking my husband, James, to jail. *He's
not a criminal,* I wanted to shout. *He's a missionary teaching
people how to live better. He's making your city a better place in
which to live.*

I thought about the happenings of the last few days.
Tomas Mendoza, a beginning preacher, was asked to stay on
the Indian reservation in Santa Catarina while the resident
missionaries, Sister Edith Cole and her helpers, went away for
the summer. Having no vehicle in which to move their things
that he and his family were leaving behind, Tomas asked his
brother, Pedro, and James to take the boxes that he left in his
house and store them for him.

Brother Harland Smith had picked up Tomas and his
family at about 4:00 a.m. Near 6:00 a.m., Pedro and James
had taken Tomas' things and stored them. *How could doing
a good deed land a man in jail?*

By the time I was over the shock, my three older children, Señora Esquier and her girls, and Señor and Señora Torres had come in to comfort me. The women were crying. I was trembling but smiling. I clenched my jaws to keep from biting my tongue. "He'll be all right. I'm going to go down right now and get him out," I mumbled through clenched teeth.

"Sister, you can't get him out. Sometimes people who have done nothing bad, but are falsely accused, stay in jail for years."

"God can do anything," I said. I was still smiling.

Señor Torres spoke up, "Sister, you are wasting your time. You have to go through the correct procedures and prove him innocent before he can be released. Even with lawyers, sometimes it takes years."

"God will help us," I replied. By now Tricia and Tim were crying. Tim hid his face in my skirt and Tricia was leaning against me. I hugged each one. Bob stood across the room in a take-charge posture with an angry fearful look in his eyes.

Señora Esquier had her arms around me. "Could you please watch the children?" I asked. They did all they could to convince me that there was no hope, but when they saw I was determined to go, she agreed to watch the children.

On the way to the jail, the Lord began forming thoughts in my mind of what I should or should not do. I should not speak Spanish. There would be less danger of being misunderstood because of my inability to use the language properly. Another reason for this would be that if they thought I couldn't understand them, they would be free to talk amongst themselves in my presence, thus permitting me to get more information. I felt confident that God would supply money for his bail, although I had only a few coins in my purse. I had heard that Mexican policemen accepted bribes and that money could get a person out of almost anything; but my trust was in God.

I parked in front of the police station, prayed again, and went into the office with assurance that everything would be okay. Walking up to the reception desk, I asked, "May I speak to the chief of police?" Promptly an interpreter came in. He was a short, fat, beady-eyed man; the chief, a big robust guy, came in behind him.

"I'm the wife of the American you have just locked up," I said. "Why is he here?"

Every policeman in the station gathered around. The ones who knew the case explained it to the others. Then the chief told the interpreter to tell me. "Your husband has stolen many things; in fact, he stole a whole house full of things." Little did he know that I understood what each of them had said.

When he had finished telling me the evil deeds of my husband, I said, "He didn't steal anything, he helped somebody move their things." Then I asked, "Now sir, can you please tell me how to get him out?"

"Yes, Madam," he answered, "You must prove him innocent." *That is what everyone is telling me,* I thought, *but how do you do that?*

"That may take a long time," I said. "Can't I post bond now?" I pleaded.

"No!" he stormed.

"But you could keep the bond money if he didn't return," I replied. "Just tell me how much you want." I said.

"NO!" he roared. "No amount of money will get him out of here!" Then he whirled himself around and walked away.

Thoughtfully I descended the steps and got into the car. I hadn't even seen James, and I had told the brethren that I would bring him home with me. I could have felt defeated, but I didn't. God had placed a confidence within my heart, so I knew God would get him out.

Questions for Discussion:
1. What does God promise us?
2. Why should we not be afraid?
3. Why were James' friends afraid?
4. How long might James be in jail?
5. How do you react when falsely accused?
(to be continued)

A TIME OF FEAR

Fear thou not; for I am with thee: be not dismayed;
for I am thy God: I will strengthen thee; yea, I
will help thee; yea, I will uphold thee with the
right hand of my righteousness. Isaiah 41:10

That evening when I arrived home from visiting James in
the Rosarito jail, Pedro's nephew was waiting for me. "Aunt
Beatrice sent me to ask if you would take some blankets for
Bro. James and Uncle Pedro," he said. "She's taking supper to
them now, but she has only enough blankets to keep herself
warm."

"What? Are they so bad they don't deserve a bed or food?"
I asked.

"The families are responsible for their needs: food, water,
and anything else they may want. I think they try to make
jail as miserable as possible. Are you able to spare a couple
blankets?"

"Well, yes. We have extra blankets." But no! I thought
to myself. *I will not take blankets. I believe they will be home
tonight.* "I'll help whatever way I can. Tell her not to worry.
They will be all right."

The boy left and I went into the house to see about my
children. The Esquier girls, Ramona and Graciela, had

made delicious large thin flour tortillas, the kind that people from Sonora make, tortillas that are patted out by hand and measure about 15 inches in diameter. Then they are cooked on a 55 gallon size barrel stove top. Graciela brought me a hot one. I quickly warmed up some refried beans and rice, and we all sat down and ate contentedly. It was the first time I had eaten that day.

My hopes were still high, but waves of doubt sometimes almost overtook me. After everyone left and I was cleaning the kitchen, a sudden FEAR gripped me! My small world was suddenly sealed in fear. *What if they couldn't come home tonight? What if they couldn't get out for a week? Or a month?? Or a year??? What would I do with four small children, the oldest being only seven? I could not leave the country and return to the states. I'd have to stay near to take James food, clean clothes, and other things when he needed them.*

By now, Rosi and Tim were asleep. I was trembling and could hardly talk; however, Bob, Tricia and I knelt on the cold cement floor beside their iron-post bunk beds. There we prayed. My prayer was much like King David's prayer in Psalms 56, although at the time I didn't realize it.

After each of the children and I had prayed, I got the Bible and read, Psalms 56:1-3. *"Be merciful unto me, O God: for man would swallow me up; he fighting daily oppresseth me. Mine enemies would daily swallow me up: for they be many that fight against me, O thou Most High. What time I am afraid, I will trust in thee."* The words, **"What time I am afraid, I will trust in thee"** stood out in bold letters. I hadn't thought of those words while I was praying.

A new determination filled my being! *How foolish it was to be afraid when all Heaven is behind me,* I thought. *I will go and take the blankets to James and Pedro in jail and maybe I can talk again to the chief.* I hurried over to get the Esquier girls to come and watch the children again.

Walking up to the reception desk again, I said, "I've brought these blankets for my husband."

The policeman on duty smiled and answered, "That's fine."

As I turned to go into the hallway that led to the jail cells, he grabbed me with one hand and the blankets in the other. "Wait!!" he shouted, blocking the passageway.

With a sweeping jerk he pulled away the blankets. He then shook them violently, one at a time, as if there were hidden weapons in some secret pocket. His eyes swept me from head to toe. It stung like sand driven by the wind. I wanted to say, *I'm not a criminal. Why can't you be a little more polite?* But I didn't. I just stood there smiling. He then threw the blankets over my shoulder and motioned where to go.

I found James and Pedro sitting cross-legged on the cold hard cement floor. They were reading the Bible together. The cell was a square room, eight feet by eight feet, about as big as a bathroom. Cement block walls were on three sides. The other side was iron bars and an iron bolted door. There was nothing in the cell, no bed, no chair, not even drinking water. James and Pedro looked so happy that I couldn't resist asking if they were enjoying their stay in the Rosarito Hilton.

"Things could be a lot worse," James answered.

I crammed the blankets, one at a time, through the bars. "I'm sure glad you brought these," Pedro said. "I am getting cold." He wrapped one around himself. James folded the other blanket into a cushion and sat on it.

We visited a few minutes and then James said, "See if Sister Esquier will let Ramona stay with you to help with the children. Here's all the money I have. Buy the children some milk. I don't know what God has in mind by putting me here, but maybe He wants me to preach to the guards and prisoners. It would be an opportunity. Tell the children to pray that I'll do whatever God wants me to do while I am in here. Goodbye now, and don't cry."

Through blinding tears, I made my way back up the hall. I stumbled down the steps and got into our car. *He is so resigned to stay in here, so happy, so satisfied with whatever comes his way,* I said to myself. *But to me this looks like a bad testimony. People who don't know him will never believe it's a false accusation. The rumor will be, 'The Church of God missionary is in jail for stealing.' That will never do! Besides, God has already given me the assurance that he will <u>not</u> stay in here.*

Questions for Discussion:
1. What would be the advantages of not serving food in jail?
2. Why did Charlotte take the blankets?
3. Why was James happy in jail?
4. What is meant by 'all heaven is behind me'?
5. What should we do when we are afraid?
6. Discuss how false rumors hurt the church.

(to be continued)

James was happy to
stay in jall if God
wanted him there..

FREEDOM!

And at midnight Paul and Silas prayed, and sang praises
unto God: and the prisoners heard them. Acts 16:25

I bolted through the door at the police station in Rosarito
Beach, Mexico. "I'm checking to see if you have decided
anything about how to get the American and his friend out of
this jail? They haven't broken a law, or done anything wrong;
they were helping Pedro's brother move."

The two policemen ignored me. All I could hear was my
heavy breathing and the scratching of the pen of the man
writing at the desk. After a long wait, the gruff-faced chief
relaxed and smiled. "So you speak Spanish?" he said. (I had
intended to not speak Spanish, but in my excitement, I had
forgotten. I was speaking Spanish!)

"Yes, there is something you can do. Bring the owner of
the stolen goods into this office. If he will testify that your
husband had permission to take the articles, then we will
release the prisoners."

"Thank you," I said, and walked out into the twilight and
got into our 1950 Chevy station wagon. I slumped over the
steering wheel and cried. *Would the old car make the trip to
Santa Catarina to get the owner?* I was thankful that James
was a good mechanic and kept our car in good running order

(whenever he had money and could get car parts). However, the car was 13 years old. The owner of the boxes was at the Indian reservation over a hundred miles away. The road to the reservation went through treacherous mountains and the road was over hardly tractable desert trails. All the roads through the loose desert sand looked the same to me. I was afraid I couldn't remember how to get there.

One time we had been lost for two days in that same desert and did without water for 17 hours. I knew that I could not find the reservation, and I knew no one in town who did know the way.

I lifted my head, dried my tears and quoted to myself, Philippians 4:13. *"I can do all things through Christ who strengthens me."* God filled me with new determination. I checked the gas gauge. It was almost on empty. I counted the money James had just given me. It was just enough to get milk for the children. I'll borrow some money to get gas, and I'll ask Pedro's brother and sister to go with me. God will lead us, I said to myself as I drove away from the police station. We will bring Tomas, the owner of the things, back with us.

The first thing I did was to get permission from Señor Miguel Esquier for his two older girls to stay overnight with my children. I then had worship with the children. I read Bible portions that would calm their fears. I told them their Daddy was content to stay in jail, if God had something for him to do there, and that he had asked them to pray for him to do God's will. We all knelt by their beds and prayed.

I tucked each one in bed and kissed them good night. Then I sat down on the cement floor beside their bunk beds to make my plans while they drifted off to sleep.

Borrowing money would be very hard, as our friends seldom had extra money. *I'll drop by and ask Pedro's brother, Lalo, and his sister, Hermelinda, to go with me while I'm out hunting money. I'm sure they will do anything I ask. Lalo has been there, at least once. Surely God will help us find it.*

When I thought the children were asleep, I went out into the big room where we had church service three times a week. In whispered tones I told my plans to the Esquier girls. While I was giving them advice about caring for the children, a pickup stopped in front of the mission house.

James met me at the door! Behind him were Pedro and his two brothers, Lalo and Gorge.

"I didn't think they could keep a good man like you in jail," I said as I hugged him. "But tell us. How did this happen? I mean, did you get released? I'm sure God didn't send an earthquake; at least, I didn't feel one. Did the warden sneak you out the back door?"

"Well, it's this way," James said. "After you left, God put quietness over the jail and the police station. It was like everyone had gone to sleep. The only noise was Pedro and me studying the Bible. I think everyone in the building could hear us reading, because the walls and floor were cement and there was nothing soft to absorb the sound. Even if they never go to church, they heard a good bit of the Bible. Then we got to singing. The hymns in that little book, *HIMNOS DE GLORIA,* are mini-sermons. I don't know which they couldn't stand, the Word of God, or our singing.

"At any rate, a man came and unlocked the bars and motioned for us to come out. We picked up our blankets and books, and we walked out to the reception desk. The chief said, 'We've decided this is no place for you two. You have been here long enough. We are dismissing all of the charges.' We said, 'Thank you,' shook his hand and walked out.

"About two blocks from the jail, Lalo picked us up. He had borrowed a pickup and was coming by to see if you would go with him to the reservation to get Tomas."

"And I was just leaving to pick up Lalo to go with me to the reservation." We laughed and I hugged James again. We bowed down on our knees and thanked the Lord for His deliverance.

A few weeks later, Señora Mendoza, the lady who had called the police, became very ill. She called for James. He visited her, and she apologized to him and then asked him to pray for her. For many weeks she suffered intensely. She had been a very cranky woman; but during those weeks she made peace with God and men.

In September, about six weeks later, while we were at the Pacoima, California camp meeting, the family called James. They told him she had died, and they wanted him to come and preach her funeral.

The whole situation made a great impression on those that knew about it.

Questions for Discussion:
1. Where did this story happen?
2. What did James and Pedro do in jail?
3. How did the cell door of the jail get open?
4. What happened to the woman who falsely accused them?
5. Did she apologize and ask for prayer?
6. What affect did this have on those who knew about it?

A Mysterious Visitor

For they all made us afraid, saying, Their hands shall be weakened from the work, that it be not done. Now therefore, O God, strengthen my hands. Nehemiah 6:9

January 1963— "Here comes Bobby. See him?" Tim called as Bobby came running down the driveway. Tim and I met him at the gate in front of our little house. Bobby showed Tim the picture he had colored in school, and he gave me the list of memory words that the first graders had to learn.

"We will study these later," I said. "First, let's go into the back yard and we'll have a snack at the picnic table. I made banana bread today and we are eating some now."

While Bobby was eating, Tim was kicking a ball against the concrete-block wall that fenced our back yard. Tricia took his list of words and began trying to read them. She very much wanted to learn to read, but she was too young to go to school. Bobby was more interested in learning about airplanes than learning words. "How can they be so big and stay in the air without anything holding them up?" he often asked.

That evening for family worship we sang: "God Will Take Care of You" written by Civilla D. Martin.

Be not dismayed what e'er betide,

God will take care of you.
Beneath his wings of love abide,
God will take care of you.
Through days of toil when heart doth fail,
God will take care of you.
When dangers fierce your paths assail,
God will take care of you.

After singing, we read from the Bible in the sixth chapter of Nehemiah. Some leaders of the neighboring nations wanted to kill Nehemiah and stop his workers from rebuilding the city walls of Jerusalem. But instead, God protected him, so he and the people in Jerusalem rebuilt the walls in record time—only fifty-two days.

"Wow! That was quick," Bobby exclaimed.

"Were the walls like the ones in our back yard?" Tricia asked.

"Oh, much, much taller," Bobby said. "They were this high." He stood on his chair and reached as high as he could. "No, they were high as the sky."

"Were they really?" Tricia asked.

"I think they were almost forty feet high and eight feet wide," I said. "Forty feet would be almost as high as four houses (the size of ours in Mexico) stacked one on top of the other. Sometimes people built little houses on top of the city walls. Remember the story of Rahab who protected the men that went as spies into the land of Canaan?"

"Her house was on the wall of Jericho," Bobby added. "It fell when the wall of Jericho came tumbling down." He tumbled off his chair onto the floor. Tim jumped on top of him and they started wrestling.

"Come boys, it's not time for play," I admonished.

"I was just showing what happened to Rahab's house," replied Bobby.

"I wish the wall behind our house was that tall. I get scared when I hear men fighting and yelling," Tricia said.

"God will take care of us," I assured her. "Remember we just sang about that. Now let's pray and then we'll get ready for bed."

Last winter, the first winter we were in Baja, each of us had been sick at one time or another. Baby Rosi had colds and fever for several months. For that reason, we moved to Pomona, California to stay during the winter months. We rented a two bedroom house next door to our close friends, John and Carolyn Sherrill, so I wouldn't feel so alone while James was staying most of the time in Mexico attending to the mission work. This week he was away.

It was easy to be afraid because a five foot cement wall was all that separated us from a tavern which was open 24 hours a day. Often we heard men shouting, sirens screaming, and saw flashing lights of police cars when they came to stop fights.

Because we had only two bedrooms, the girls, who were smaller, slept in the living room on the sofa. After worship each night I unfolded the sofa and made it into a bed. One side of this rectangular shaped house was the living room, kitchen and dining area. The other side had the two bedrooms with the bathroom between them. Whoever was on the sofa could see anyone coming in the back door although they could not see the door itself.

One evening, after everyone had their bath, we prayed. Then I tucked the children into their beds and kissed them good night. Before long I was stretched out on a big bed by myself and sound asleep.

Sometime later in the night, I was awakened by Tricia screaming. She came running into my bedroom, shouting, "Mamma! Mamma! The devil—the devil—the devil's coming in the door!"

I awoke and putting my arms around her, I said, "Don't cry. You were just dreaming."

"No," she said, "the devil came in the back door. I saw him."

"Everything is all right. No one is here. See," I said, pointing into the dining room, "there is no one in there."

She insisted that an old man with cowboy boots and a straw hat had come in. I couldn't console her, so I put her into my bed supposing it was just another one of her bad dreams. Then, just to feel more secure myself, I went to check the back door.

The door was ajar! So she had seen a man come in!

"Thank you, God for waking her up. Thank You for protecting us," I said.

By now I was shaking and trembling with fright. I checked the door lock. That's when I saw signs where the wood had been chipped away around the lock, making it possible to open. I pulled the table against the door, then I lined up chairs against it until they touched the opposite wall. *Now to get the door open a chair will have to be crushed or a hole knocked into the wall,* I thought. After that I went into the living room and I pushed the sewing machine and the sofa in front of the living room door.

I looked down at little Rosi sleeping peacefully on the sofa that I had just dragged against the door. *She is too close to the door,* I thought, so I carried her to my bed. Even with all my blocking of doors and getting my girls near me, it was awhile before I calmed down and went back to sleep.

The following morning I had to tell the whole story when the boys asked, "Who moved our furniture around in the night?"

Questions for Discussion:
1. Why did Tricia wish for a high wall around their house?
2. What song did they sing during family worship?
3. What two city walls did they read about?
4. Why were they sometimes afraid?
5. How did God protect the family?
6. Talk about a time when God protected you.

THE TORNADO

The LORD is slow to anger, and great in power,
and will not at all acquit the wicked: the LORD
hath his way in the whirlwind . . . Nahum 1:3

On a trip to the Santa Catarina Indian Reservation, we stopped near Ojos Negros to visit a family who had recently built a new brick house. Later the following weekend when Brother Harland Smith stopped to visit us, James told him about our visit.

"Wonderful! I've wanted to stop, but I just haven't found time. So they were interested?" asked Brother Harland.

"Yes, they asked for a Bible, but I had already given away all the Bibles you had brought us," James answered.

Brother Harland was happy to take them a Bible, and he kept visiting them on his weekend trips out into the desert. One Sunday evening he brought us the good news that the lady of the house, Señora Gomez, had surrendered her life to God. "Please, be sure and visit her whenever you are out that way," he said.

Later when Brother Smith was constructing the Church of God Sunset Guest Home in Pacoima, California, he couldn't come to Mexico as often. We were taking up the slack and making more trips into the desert to keep in touch with the contacts. Whenever possible, we stopped to visit the lady in the new brick house. One evening James asked her husband if he felt a need to be saved. "No," he answered, "I see no need of wasting my time with religion. It's all right for the Señora if it makes her feel better. You can come and sing for her." Having said that, he put his straw sombrero on and escaped out the door. Soon we heard his tractor motor start and listened as he drove away.

He was usually away when we came to visit Señora Gomez. One evening he happened to be there, and he reproved us, saying, "You folks are too young to be wasting your time like this. You should be working and laying up money so your children will have a good start when they are grown."

"Maybe you are right. However, we think helping others have an eternal home in heaven is far more important. Everything on this earth will be burned up one of these days," James said.

"Maybe you think so, however I want to be the owner of a lot of land that I can pass on to my sons," Señor Gomez replied.

Several weeks passed and we hadn't visited the family. The next time we stopped Mrs. Gomez said sadly, "My husband thinks I should be doing something more productive than studying the Bible."

Later, Brother Harland shared with us that when he stopped by, he found the same rejection. He said that he cautioned Señor Gomez to not make a god of this world. Nevertheless, Señor Gomez just laughed and boasted, "One of these days, I'll be the richest farmer in the Ojos Negro Valley."

"That is sad, for God's Word says, 'Lay not up for yourselves treasures upon this earth . . . But lay up for yourselves treasures in heaven . . .'" James added.

"Yes, it is dangerous to reject the Gospel," Bro. Harland agreed.

A few weeks later, on a trip to the desert, we were shocked to see their new place looked ragged and abandoned. We wondered if something had happened to Mr. Gomez. We asked at the general store in Ojos Negros, and they told us that a small tornado had passed through and had frightened Señor Gomez away. We checked the house and it was damaged. Some windows were broken, some roof decking was torn away from one corner of the roof, and door facings were hanging loose.

Another month or so later, as we drove by, we saw clothes hanging on the line. We stopped to see who was living there. Señora Gomez greeted us at the door with a happy face and hugs. Señor Gomez was sitting at the table in front of the refrigerator. He looked much older than he did the day he had reproved James for not building up wealth for his children.

We tried to show concern for his loss without seeming nosy. Señor Gomez quickly admitted his mistake. "Si, God punished me for my haughty attitude and for making gold my god. I told you I planned to buy more ranch land. The day before the tornado, I went to the bank in Ensenada and took out all my money. I had it right on top of that refrigerator." He turned around and pointed to the top of the refrigerator. "That night a tornado came through. The wind blew the window open and sucked the money out. I went out the following morning and looked everywhere for it, but I only found a few bills. I know God was angry with me. All my savings from my hard work blew away in the wind."

"The Bible tells us that the 'Lord has his way in the whirlwind,'" James said.

Questions for Discussion:

1. Why did Señora Gomez want a Bible?
2. What did Señor Gomez love most?
3. For what was he saving his money?
4. What happened to his money?
5. Why did he think God took his money?
6. Who has his way in the whirlwind?

Ramona Visits President Lopez Mateos

Be strong and of a good courage; be not afraid,
neither be thou dismayed: for the Lord thy God is
with thee whithersoever thou goest. Joshua 1:9b

I was scrubbing clothes on the back side of the mission house
when I saw the next door neighbor's daughter coming home
from school. "Hi Ramona," I said, "I've been told that you
have the highest scores in your grade. Congratulations! Isn't
it exciting to be at the head of your graduation class?"

"Yes, I am happy about that, but, but, but," she stuttered
and started crying.

"Now what has happened? Won't you come in and tell me
about it?" I dried my hands on my apron, and opening the
door, I motioned for her to go in.

As we stepped inside, Tricia came running and threw her
arms around Ramona. Ramona smiled and hugged Tricia.

We sat down facing each other on one of the wooden
church benches that filled our living room. Tricia sat between
us while Ramona explained, "President Lopez Mateos has
offered the top students in every state a three day vacation to
the capital. Each sixth grade student who has the top scores
in their school is supposed to have a chance to compete with

other top students. However, because our school is a Christian school we were not notified about it. I don't think that is fair, do you?"

"No, it isn't fair," I said. "But Ramona, no one is treated fairly all the time. We all have to learn to accept both fair and unfair treatments." Tears rolled down her cheeks while I was speaking. "I know it is hard, but it will help you face other problems in life if you learn to forgive and let go. God will help you." Then I prayed for God to comfort her.

The following day, her mother, Christina explained to me, "President Mateos is trying to help the people of our country. He has opened up and given away more *ejido* land than any other president since Lazaro Cardenas. I understand that his father died when he was young. His widowed mother, a school teacher, directed an orphanage in Mexico City to make a living for their family. He studied using a scholarship program. Therefore he wants to help the poor children who wish to be successful, and he wishes to motivate all children to study. Each state has been divided into sections, ours has thirteen. The top student from each school is supposed to take a test. The boy or girl who scores highest on this test will represent our section and will get to tour our nation's capital and have dinner with President and Señora Lopez Mateos."

"And the church school was not allowed to participate?" I asked.

"Our school was not notified. Maybe it was an oversight, or maybe because it is a Christian school. The school director is going to the Educational Department to see what can be done about it."

About a week later, early on Saturday morning, Ramona's father knocked on our door. "Sorry to bother you so early, but we need prayer. Ramona is going this morning into Tijuana to take a test. Please pray that God will keep her calm and help her know how to answer the questions."

"Come in," I said; then I asked, "Is this the testing to see if she will qualify to visit the president?"

"Oh, *sí, sí* (yes, yes)," Ramona said with a big smile. We knelt and prayed and then laid hands on her and prayed again.

Another week passed while we anxiously waited for the results of the testing. When the news came, it was both sweet and bitter. Ramona's scores were the very highest. However, since she took the test alone in a calm uninterrupted environment, her score could not be compared with those of students testing together in a large group.

"That isn't fair!," we all said at the same time.

"No, but life isn't fair," Ramona reminded me, with tears in her eyes. We all prayed both for Ramona's comfort and for justice.

Finally, Ramona was chosen as the student for our section of the state. A few weeks later she was traveling to Mexico City with twelve other students and chaperones from Baja California Norte. They rode all day and all that night. The following day they arrived in Mexico City at about 8:00 p.m.

The following morning they toured the city, seeing many historical and famous things. In the evening there was a formal dinner and a dance at the hotel. Ramona ate dinner, excused herself and went to her room. "This will be a good time to be alone and read my Bible and pray," she said, as she entered the room where the girls were staying. "Tomorrow we will visit the university, the Aztec Indian Ruins, and the Chapultepec Park and Zoo. By going to bed early, I'll have plenty of energy for all the walking."

On the third day, they visited the Cathedral of Mexico City, the Nacional Monte de Piedad, the Nacional Palacio, and the Old Portal de Mercaderas.

Finally the big evening came when they would dine with the President. The girls' room was alive with excitement.

Some were putting on beautiful clothing, others were having their hair combed by the women chaperones, while still others had gone to the beauty shops to have theirs done.

"Aren't you going to have something done to your hair?" one of the girls asked Ramona.

Ramona had already been thinking about her hair. She had decided the way she usually combed her hair was the way Christ wanted her to comb it. "I guess not," she answered.

"Are you really going to see the President in the plain way you are dressed?" asked another. "You can borrow my makeup. It will make you look better."

"No, Gracias" she answered again, "I never wear makeup."

When Ramona was ready to go, the girl who shared her bed, said, "I'd be ashamed to go dressed the way you are."

Another added, "Your dress is much too long and out of style."

Ramona said nothing. She wanted to please Jesus more than to look beautiful to the world.

Many, many students were at the dinner that evening. Ramona, with twelve other students from Baja California Norte sat together at their table. After the meal was finished, President Lopez Mateos announced, "I will ask two students from each state to come forward to receive a trophy and honors for their state. I will call the name of the state and then two names, one boy and one girl. When I call your name please come up onto the platform to receive the honors for your state."

First one state and then another was called. Everyone was excited; each was hoping they would be called. At Ramona's table some whispered among themselves about who he might call. Two more states were called, and then, "Baja California Norte." Everyone listened excitedly. "Will Jose Gonzales Perez and Ramona Esquier Villa please come forward?"

"Ramona!" the girls gasped.

Jose followed Ramona up the three steps to the platform. "I want my picture taken with you," President Lopez Mateos said to Ramona. "You are a perfect example for others to follow." As he said that, he put his arm over her shoulder and motioned for the photographer to snap the photo.

Ramona returned home rejoicing in her heart that God had given her strength to be true to Him even in unusual circumstances.

On her fifteenth birthday, Ramona received a package from President Lopez Mateos. It was a thirteen by fifteen inch framed photograph of Ramona with the President. An enclosed letter read:

Happy birthday to a wonderful girl! We will always remember you.

President and Señora Lopez Mateos

Questions for Discussion:
1. Why was Ramona sad?
2. What should we do when not treated fairly?
3. Who helped Ramona make good decisions?
4. How did Ramona dress when dining with the president?
5. What did the president say about Ramona?
6. Have you had to stand alone for Christ?

The Missing Pony Tail

Likewise ye younger, submit yourselves unto the
elder. Yea, all of you be subject one to another, and
be clothed with humility: for God resisteth the
proud, and giveth grace to the humble. I Peter 5:5

Tomas Mendoza was our first mission worker in Rosarito
Beach. He began preaching within the first year after meeting
us. The following summer he moved to the Indian Reservation
to stay in the mission house while Sis. Edith Cole went home
to attend the Monark Springs Camp Meeting. We were happy
for him, but we also missed him tremendously. After living
there in Santa Catarina, he moved down into Valle Trinidad
and raised up a large congregation there.

One day in the spring he brought us a young goat. I
suppose he thought that we would make barbecue goat for
Easter Sunday dinner. Instead of barbecuing the goat, we
made it our pet. During the day, while we could watch the
goat, we tied it out in the field near the house so it could eat
the tender spring grass. At night we kept it inside the house
where it was protected from thieves or hungry dogs. We
rearranged the church benches to make a little corral in one
corner of our chapel-living room. Each evening before dark,
the children brought the goat in and put it to bed.

Our goat soon learned to love the children. He ate from their hands. He followed them like a dog when they went to the store. He played "king on the mountain," butting heads with both Bobby and Timmy.

One Sunday morning after bathing Rosi, I said, "Be very careful and don't get your dress dirty. You are all ready for church."

"I be careful, Mama," she promised. "Me no get dirty."

As I was gathering up my clean clothes, I called to Tricia. "Watch Rosi while I am getting ready. She just went outside."

A few moments later, Tricia opened the door and called, "She's out there petting the goat. I told her no, but she said, 'Goaty no get me dirty. Goaty clean Goaty.' When I try to pull her away, she screams."

"Then just leave her alone, but don't let her play in the dirt. I'll be right out." James had taken the boys and had gone to pick up the people from the Tomato Ranch out north of town. I had no other helper. I splashed and scrubbed as quickly as possible, but before I could get dressed, I heard Rosi crying. The sound was getting louder as she was coming in.

Soon she was inside and her crying was echoing off the cement block walls. She was trying to say something. I listened carefully. In between sobs, she was saying, "Goaty, mean Goaty. Me hair! Goaty Me hair!"

I peeked out from behind my bath curtain. There stood Rosi holding a few strands of her hair. Her pony tail was gone! "What happened to your pony tail?" I shouted.

"Goaty eat me tail!" she cried.

"And the other one?" I asked. "Turn your head around." The three inch pony tail on the other side of her head was still in place. The goat had eaten the other one right down to her scalp. "Well, you should have obeyed Tricia when she tried to pull you away from the goat," I said sternly.

I had trouble keeping the children's attention during class that morning. All the girls wanted to look at Rosi's strange hairdo. It was short against her head on one side and three inches long on the other.

On a Friday night, a few weeks later, Brother Harland Smith stopped by on his way to El Alamo. As usual he arrived about midnight. He would not take one of our beds and we didn't have a spare one. Using his flash light, he found an empty spot among the benches and threw his sleeping bag on the floor. Then he crawled in and went to sleep. We had no electricity, nor any outside lights other than the moon and stars. This night the moon was not shining at all. It was very dark.

Goaty, as Rosi called him, loved people. It seems the poor goat tried to snuggle up next to Bro. Smith, who was snoring beside him.

The following morning Brother Harland said, "Last night I thought sure this house was full of rats. I kept hearing noises but I was so tired I couldn't wake up. I would try to open my eyes and find my flash light, but my eyes were stuck closed. Finally sometime this morning, I felt what I thought was a warm breath on my face. Quickly I opened my eyes and I saw a goat looking down at me. He must have been trying to squeeze his head between the boards on the back of the bench."

"It's a good thing he couldn't reach your hair," I said, "That goat likes to eat hair."

Brother Harland rubbed his hand over his thinning hair and said, "He wouldn't have found much on my head. However, it doesn't feel like there are any less than there were before I went to sleep."

"Just be thankful. A few days ago that goat ate Rosi's hair right off her head!"

"Oh no! You have to be kidding," he said.

"No! I'm not. Just wait till you see her."

Questions for Discussion:
1. What animal became the children's pet?
2. Why was Tricia watching Rosi?
3. Why should Rosi have obeyed Tricia?
4. Did God say that we should obey our elders?
5. Do you obey when an older sibling is caring for you?

10 Hamburgers for $1.00

. . . Go thou to the sea, and cast a hook, and take up the fish . . . and when thou hast opened his mouth, thou shall find a piece of money: that take, and give unto them for me and thee. Matthew 17:27

"Wake-up," I called to our four sleeping children. "Help me get ready; we are going to the Pacoima, California camp meeting today. Your Daddy is already checking the car."

Bobby wrinkled his face and opened one eye. "I thought I heard Dad say we didn't have enough money to buy gas to go to Pacoima."

"We have decided to trust God to get us there," I answered.

"What can I do to help get ready?" asked seven-year-old Tricia.

"Me help, too," said Tim as he was climbing out of bed.

"You both can help scrub your dirty clothes." I answered. "We will wash them in the washing machine at the campground. However, each of you will need to scrub the dirt out of your socks. And you boys get your jeans scrubbed. We can't put them in the machine until the worst of the dirt is out."

Bobby quickly got into his clothes, went outside, and began drawing buckets of water out of the hand dug well.

"We'll need two tubs of water, each about half full so two of you can wash at the same time," I told Bobby. Since he was only nine years old, it took all his strength to lift the heavy buckets of water. When I saw him struggling, I cautioned, "Don't let the bucket get so full. Jerk it up when you first feel it getting heavy before it has time to fill all the way to the top."

Rosi came toddling out of the bed room, "Me wash, too," she said.

"Tricia, hurry over and borrow Sis. Esquier's scrub board, if she isn't using it." While I was getting breakfast, the children were each scrubbing out the worst of the dirt from their clothes. We put the white clothes into two five-gallon buckets and the dark colored clothes into a round tub. The dry clothes that weren't so dirty went into the pillow cases and a laundry bag.

I was surprised that most of the clothes were ready to go by the time I had breakfast ready. Tricia helped me wash and put away the breakfast dishes while Bobby helped James clean out our station wagon.

The girls were dressing as quickly as I was laying out the clean clothes to wear on the trip. There were no decisions as to which clothes we were taking. We had only three changes of presentable clothes. One set was dirty. We would wear one outfit. The other clean ones were put into suitcases, along with Bibles, notebooks, and a few toys. Our two new suitcases were gifts from Brother Ed Sorrell.

We all worked together like ants do, and we were packed and ready to go before noon. Since we had no money to buy lunch, I cooked a pan of rice and warmed up the beans so we could eat just before leaving. "That should keep you satisfied until we eat supper at the camp ground," I said.

"Will we be there for supper?" Bobby asked.

"We should, unless something unusual happens," I answered.

During all the twenty years that James and I lived in Mexico, we anxiously looked forward to the Pacoima meetings. They were like a breath of fresh air, a spiritual feast, and a spring of living water to drink from. If at all possible, we would go each September and December.

This year we thought it was impossible. However, as the time grew nearer and nearer, our desires to be there grew stronger and stronger, until at last we decided to go by faith.

As we pulled into a gas station in Chula Vista, California, James said, "I sure wish I had more money. I know this will not buy enough gas to get us there."

"We will have to trust God to stretch it," I said.

He bought gas with all the money we had. "Maybe if I adjust the timing we can get a few more miles out of the gasoline," he said. "I have already put in all the gasoline-additive that I had." He drove our station wagon a small distance away from the pumps and parked it so he could adjust the timing.

While he was working under the hood of the car, I let our four children play around outside. I was watching what they were doing when I saw Tim go into the public telephone booth. He put the receiver to his ear and was pretending he was talking on the phone. I nodded for Bobby to go get him. When Tim saw Bob coming, he slammed the receiver down on the hook and ran.

The hard slam on the receiver caused a great deal of change to come tumbling out. Bob shouted, "Mom, come here quick. Look at all this money!"

I jumped out and hurried to the phone booth. Quarters, dimes, and nickels filled Bob's hands and some lay on the floor. It never occurred to any of us that the money belonged to someone else. We thought God put it there just for us.

James backed up to the pump again and added more gas to the gas tank. When he told the attendant what had happened, the attendant said, "Someone probably hurried away and didn't wait for their change."

We pulled out onto Interstate 5 and headed north toward Pacoima without the fear of running out of gas. About an hour later, somewhere near Santa Ana, James shouted, "Look at that sign!"

A big sign read, "10 HAMBURGERS for $1.00." James whipped off the Interstate and bought 10 hamburgers with money he had saved from the coins we had found.

The children were jubilant! We sat around a table on the patio shaded by a big red, white, and blue striped umbrella as if we were as rich as any family in America. And were we not? We had a rich heavenly Father!

We had more hamburgers than people, but don't you think they were thrown away. All ten hamburgers were eaten.

We sang and played games the remaining distance to Pacoima. God also blessed us to get through Los Angles just ahead of the heavy rush hour traffic, thus arriving in time for a splendid campground supper! However, we were still full of ten cent hamburgers.

Questions for Discussion:
1. Where did the family want to go?
2. Why did they think they couldn't go?
3. Why did they decide to go?
4. How did the children help get ready?
5. Where did they get money for gas and hamburgers?
6. Has God enabled you do something you could not do?

A HEALING MIRACLE

Bless the LORD, O my soul, and forget not all
his benefits: Who forgiveth all thine iniquities;
who healeth all thy diseases; Psalms 103:2, 3

September 1965—"Tomorrow is our first day of school,"
Tricia said as we were laying out clothes for her and her two
brothers to wear. "I'm so happy to be going to school. I'll have
new friends, and I think I am really going to like Mrs. Kerr."

"I'm sure she will be a good teacher, and yes, you will have
friends. The Bible tells us in Proverbs 18:24 that, 'A man that
hath friends must show himself friendly: and there is a friend
that sticketh closer than a brother.' You are friendly, so you
will have friends. You also have the Friend who is closer to
you than your brother, so you already have one very special
friend."

"Is that Friend Jesus?" asked Tricia.

"Yes, that friend is Jesus."

"I have Him in my heart because I am saved."

"Yes, and saved from what?"

"I'm saved from the bad things that I have done."

"Yes, you are saved from sin. Jesus will help you at school
to be good, kind and not do any evil."

"I hope He will," Tricia said kind of wishfully.

"Why don't we pray and ask God to help you, and while we are praying, let us pray for Bobby that he will also be allowed to start school."

"What is keeping him from starting when Timmy and I start?"

"He has that awful sore on his neck. You know the big, red, yucky hole. It is an infection and it could spread to other children. If I could cover it with a bandage it would help, but it's almost impossible without wrapping a gauze all the way around his neck, and you know your brother would not go to school with a bandage like that."

"I know he wouldn't," Tricia said. When she prayed, she asked God to help her to be kind to others at school and to not be ashamed that she was a Christian. Then she asked God to heal the sore on Bobby's neck.

That evening after their Daddy came home from work, they ate supper, and then during family worship, they prayed again for Bobby.

The following morning I had to take James to his place of work in downtown San Diego and then get back to the children's school in El Cajon by 8:30 a.m. At six o'clock, I was packing lunches and preparing breakfast while each child dressed and combed his hair. I was still wondering if Bobby would have to return home and stay until the sore was healed.

"Hurry," I called, "breakfast is on the table." First one, and then another, came to eat while waiting a turn to enter the bathroom. No one complained about taking turns using the bathroom. After living for three years without an inside bathroom, they were all thankful to have just one.

I held baby Leah on one hip as I placed a plate of toast on the table. "Be careful and don't get jelly on your shirt," I cautioned Timmy. "Watch out!" I shouted as a glass of orange juice toppled. James caught it before it spilled on Tricia's clean dress.

"Here, Rosi, eat this egg." I placed a plate in front of her.

"And here are your lunches," I said, setting four sack lunches on the cabinet beside the sink. "Your name is on your sack. Each one must be responsible for his own lunch."

At last, all seven of us were in the car and headed toward San Diego. James drove while I combed Rosi's hair and checked over the boys. Then I smoothed out the wrinkles in the girl's dresses and wiped the crumbs from their faces with a napkin. At last they were presentable. I took a deep breath and leaned back in the seat.

At that moment I thought again about the sore. "Oh, Bobby, let me see your neck," I said as I turned to look at him in the back seat. He turned around so I could see his neck. I gasped loudly!

"What's happened now? Did you leave something important at home?" James asked

"No, it is Bobby's neck. The sore is gone!"

"What? That ugly sore is gone?"

"Yes, it's gone!"

"Let me see," Tricia said, turning Bobby so his back was toward her.

"Really?" Bobby asked. "Is it gone?"

"Yes!" I said again.

"I didn't wash my neck because I didn't want it to start bleeding."

"Well, it won't bleed again. Only a pink spot is there to remind us of where it was."

Questions for Discussion:
1. Why would Tricia have friends?
2. Why might Bobby not get to enter school?
3. What special problem did the family pray about?

4. Name some things for which the family was thankful.
5. What was on Bobby's neck where the sore had been?
6. Talk about the times God has healed you.

Shoes for Tim

How beautiful are the feet of them that
preach the gospel of peace, and bring glad
tidings of good things! Romans 10:15b

From the window above the kitchen sink, I saw the yellow school bus stop at the bottom of the hill. I could plainly see the writing on its side, San Diego Unified School District. Three of our five children, Bobby, Tricia, Timmy and two neighbor children got off the bus. Tricia was dangling a letter in her hand as she raced with Bobby up the hill.

"Here is a letter from Tim's teacher," she said. "Mrs. Kerr gave it to me."

I laid down the potato I was peeling and read the letter.

Dear Parent,

May 2 will be the May Day Celebration at the El Cajon Grade School. It will be for kindergarten through second grade. All students must wear "dress-up" clothes such as is worn for church on Sunday. Girls must wear dress shoes and boys must wear "black only" dress shoes.

Place: School Patio

Time: 1:30 to 2:30 p.m.

Please be present to see your child perform.

"Won't it be fun?" Tricia asked. "I get to lead our class."

"Oh, I'm glad Mrs. Kerr chose you. I know you will do your job well."

"School is so much fun. I just love going to school," Tricia said as she danced around in excitement. "But Mommy, why are you looking so sad? Don't you think it will be fun?"

"Oh, yes! It is just that—that—Tim has no black shoes, and we used all of our money paying the house rent. Daddy won't be getting any more money until after the program. But let's not worry about it."

"Oh, I won't," she said, as she picked up Leah who was crawling toward her.

Our youngest daughter, Leah, had been born August 7, 1965, at the mission house in Rosarito Beach, Baja California, Mexico. A doctor had walked two miles from the Red Cross station downtown to come and deliver our baby. Sister Virginia Whittenborn came and stayed for two weeks. She did the cooking and caring for the older four children.

The mission house had no inside water or bathroom. We had to go outside, around the house and across the yard whenever we needed to use the bathroom. We had a hand dug well in the back yard. To get water, we hooked a rope to a bucket, lowered it into the well, and after it filled, we pulled the heavy bucket full of water up by the rope. There was no electricity for a washing machine. Cloth diapers and all other clothes had to be washed by hand. Besides that, we had church meetings three times a week in our home which caused a lot of extra work for me, the homemaker.

I wasn't very strong after Leah's birth so we decided to move across the border where we could enjoy more sanitary conditions for our newborn and would have an inside bathroom, hot and cold water, and electricity in the house. These things would make life easier until I could regain some strength. We rented a three bedroom house from Mr. and Mrs. L. Newton. They became great friends and gave us offerings for the work in Mexico.

James took only a part time job in San Diego so he would still have time to visit and teach at the mission in Rosarito. This new residence was also nearer the dental school where James was studying Practical Dentistry.

We enrolled the children in the El Cajon school: Timmy in kindergarten, Tricia in second grade, and Bobby in the fourth grade. Sending the children to school was a challenge for me because in Mexico I didn't have to keep them well dressed. All through that school year our children looked as well dressed as the other children, for which I was thankful.

Now Tim needed black dress shoes and we didn't have money to buy them. That night in family worship we told God of our need. A few days later we received a package in the mail. We opened it and there were black shoes that fit Tim's feet. Who were they from? We never knew. Who knew that Tim needed black shoes? We never knew. Except of course, God knew.

Altogether it was a fun year for us. We made new friends and enjoyed activities in the San Diego area.

Questions for Discussion:
1. What did Tim need for the school program?
2. Why couldn't they buy new shoes?
3. Why was the family living in El Cajon?

4. How did he get new shoes for the program?
5. Name a time when God supplied something you needed.

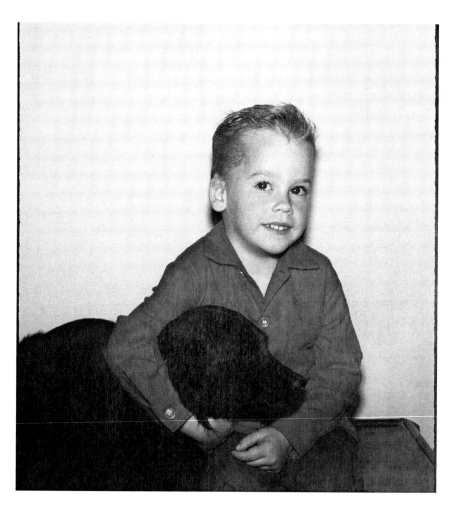

A Great Christmas

Therefore all things whatsoever ye would that men should
do to you, do ye even so to them. Matthew 7:12a

Christmas Day 1964, the year before we moved to El Cajon.
I heard a gentle tapping on our back door. When I opened
it our neighbor, Señor Torres, was standing there. He looked
exhausted and a little pale. I wondered if he was sick and
wanted James to take him to the doctor. "May I speak with
Hermano Jaime?" (Brother James) he asked rather shyly.

James was in the bedroom with the children. They had
just finished opening their Christmas presents. When James
heard Señor Torres, he came in and asked how he could help.

"I know it's a very cold day and it's Christmas morning
but we've spent a terrible night thinking about our two boys
and wondering if they will have a decent meal today. My
poor wife cried most of the night. I heard that someone saw
my boys in Tijuana a couple days ago. I was just wondering
if you could find it in your heart to take me to Tijuana and
help me look for my sons."

James turned and looked at me. I had just said, "It's so
nice to have a day together. We seldom have time alone with
our own little family." I nodded my approval and then added,
"Christmas is a time for showing love."

"Yes, I will take you," James told him. He slipped on his heavy coat, took a few things out of our Chevy station wagon and they were on their way to look for Señor Torres sons, Hector and Arthur.

Our children were pretty disappointed when they realized their Dad would be gone on Christmas Day. When they complained, I said, "Christmas is really a time of giving and doing for others. Christ left his home in heaven and came to this earth. He did it for us, so we should be able to sacrifice for others." They seemed satisfied with my little sermon and went back into the bedroom to play.

I fought back tears when I saw how willingly they conformed. I asked God to bless them. I was struggling myself to be content. Minutes before Señor Torres came, I was so happy. Now, James was gone and we were again alone.

The church had built a mission house in Rosarito while we were living those few months in Pomona. Now we were living in it. Although it was much larger and would someday be much better than the little house where we were before, it was more dreary. In fact, it was the most depressing place that I have ever lived. The walls were gray cement blocks, the floor was gray cement, the window openings were covered with black tar paper, and the dividing walls between the two bedrooms were also made of black tar paper. The unfinished wood ceiling was glorious to look at because it afforded a little color. However, it was impossible to get much work done with my eyes on the ceiling.

To make matters worse, we had received only $10.00 to buy presents for the children. We bought mostly necessities: combs, tooth-brushes, tooth paste, perfumed bath soap (that Rosi and Tricia loved), notebooks, a coloring book and crayons, pencils, and a ball. My spirit was low, but I tried to make the children happy. Yesterday I had bought a chicken to bake and a few other things we seldom enjoyed, and I had made a pumpkin pie. Even in our lack, we had more than most of our neighbors which helped to alleviate the depression.

We anxiously waited for James to return. Every time the children heard a car, they rushed to open the door to see if it was him. (The only way to see the driveway was to open the North door, since our window openings were covered.) We played *Hide the Thimble*. We pushed the church benches against the walls and played a form of *Blind Man's Bluff*. I told them stories but even so, the day was so long. Finally at about four o'clock, he came home.

We all rushed to the door. James didn't have to say anything. The happy look on his face told us that the boys were home for Christmas. It was the first time in four years.

"After we found the boys, I went across to the mail box," James said. "We received a check that was sent to buy candy and fruit for the children."

"Oh, good," I said, "Now we have some things to give them. I was so sad to not have anything to give the poor children, because what we give them might be the only treats that some of them would get. But Christmas dinner is ready so let's eat."

"Okay!" shouted the children.

After dinner, while Tricia and I cleaned the kitchen, James and the other children carried in the things that he had purchased: a huge box of oranges, two large bags of wrapped candy, a large bag of roasted peanuts, and some little sacks. It was almost five o'clock and service started at 6:00 p.m. James disappeared into the bedroom to pray and get prepared for the Christmas meeting.

I opened the little sacks and stood them on a bench. Rosi dropped one orange in each sack. Tricia and Tim each put a handful of peanuts in the bags. Since Bobby was very detailed and careful, his job was to see that each sack had the same amount of candy. He started out putting three pieces in each sack. After he had put candy in every sack, he had a lot of candy left, so he started over again, putting one more piece in each sack. Again he had candy left so he dropped two more piece in each sack. After that, he had only a few pieces left so he divided those between his siblings and himself.

We put the benches back in their proper places and then pulled the kitchen table against the south wall and arranged the sacks on it. We swept the floor. I had made a large curtain from bed-sheets. We pulled the curtain across the room to hide the kitchen stove, the sink, and our kitchen cabinets, which were open shelves made from one by twelve inch boards placed on stacked cement blocks. Using straight pins we fastened beautifully painted pictures of Mary, Joseph, baby Jesus, three shepherds and the three wise men, a cow and two sheep onto the curtain. Everything was in order when the people started coming in.

No one in the congregation had a telephone but news about the boys had gotten around. Every year we had a Christmas service, but this year a spirit of gratitude ignited it. The Christmas Carols rang as did those the angels sang that first Christmas night. Some people were laughing, some were crying, others were quietly drinking in the blissful peace, as James told the story of Jesus. After we dismissed, every child received a sack of goodies.

Questions for Discussion:
1. Give two reasons why the family was happy.
2. Did they willingly conform to what happened?
3. Why was the Torres family sad?
4. Should we be willing to help others at all times?
5. What kind of Christmas did it turn out to be?
6. What has been your best Christmas?

Also by Charlotte Huskey

Mabel

Subtitled - A Demonstration of the Power of God's Word.

This is the first in a series of Family Devotional. Our Father in Heaven, a sequel to Mabel, is to be printed in 2017.

Acknowledgments

This book has been successfully completed by God's grace and the help and inspiration from our church family. Many encouraged me to record our experiences because they believed the world should know about these recent miracles of God that happened to our family on the mission field in Baja California, Mexico.

I especially wish to acknowledge the late Brother Harland Smith—a spiritual giant full of the Holy Spirit. His companionship, fatherly wisdom, and constant support kept us stable as we took baby steps in our new adventure of living by faith. His contagious, energetic spirit filled us with hope and courage while we were growing in our calling to be missionaries.

I also wish to thank those who helped me with writing and correcting the manuscript, a few of which were: Tricia Bell, Nicole Elwell, Roberta Gaines, Lindsey Gellenbeck, Karen Goltry, Marlana Hale, Sandra Melot, Irma Sallee, Clifford and Patsy Smith, and Nelda Sorrell. I also wish to thank my children Bobby, Tricia, Tim, and Rosie, who reminded me of the details in these incidents.

Last, but not least, I thank my husband, James Huskey. It was through his unwavering faith in God and his desire to do God's will that we encountered these situations and were able to experience these miracles.

Gratefully, Charlotte Huskey

About the Author

Charlotte has been involved with children all her adult life: teaching, directing VBS, organizing camps, conducting Bible Clubs, rearing six biological children, foster parenting and editing children's Sunday school material. For fifteen years she wrote children's weekly Bible Lessons with a corresponding illustrative story for the Church of God Sunday School magazine.

She has published hundreds of short, character-building stories; two book-length serial stories, *The What Would Jesus Do Club and The Nutty Nutritional Club*; plus book-length biographies of Ahn Ei Shook, Lillian Thrasher (The Nile Mother) and Jaya Kollipara.

Charlotte is a lifelong student of family life, continually researching and writing about child training and family issues. After Charlotte married missionary dentist, James Huskey, they did evangelism and humanitarian work in Mexico for twenty-three years. She is currently writing more stories about their missionary experience and about her childhood growing up on a farm in Oregon.

Edwards Brothers Malloy
Thorofare, NJ USA
October 11, 2016